Speaking to the Heart

What Prophetic Art is, What it Looks Like, and How it is Used

Lynn Zuk-Lloyd

With Contributions from 50 Prophetic Artists

PromiseGarden.com

Speaking to the Heart: What Prophetic Art is, What it Looks Like, and How it is Used.
©2014 Lynn Zuk-Lloyd. All rights reserved.

Foreword by Bob Hay.
Introductory information, book design and compilation by Lynn Zuk-Lloyd.

Published 2014 by PromiseGarden.com
P.O. Box 638, Warrenville, IL 60555
www.promisegarden.com
books@promisegarden.com

ISBN: 978-0-9913959-0-3

The utmost care has been taken to insure accuracy in the information the artists submitted for this book, and to show their art in the best possible way. The views and opinions expressed in this book are not necessarily the views and opinions of the author and publisher. Color variations may occur from book to book as a result of the printing process.

What People Are Saying About This Book

This book is a forerunner in its day; the explanations of each artist gives real heart to its pages. Very well done! Can't wait for the next one! — Brenda Tarasenko, *Artist and Facilitator*

This book is a wonderful testimony of God's creativity revealed through His beloved people! The beautiful differences represent God's uniqueness and love! The ages represented, also spoke volumes to me as to how HE loves to bless and use His "children." Lynn did a beautiful job of putting this book together! — Matthew C Lawlor, *Follower of Jesus Christ*

I can see the hand of Jesus on this book. You will be blessed by the amazing art and stories this book contains. — Lyn Rowley, *Gifted Craftswomen*

Lynn Zuk-Lloyd has gathered a talented group of artists from a broad section of visual art — all ages, from around the country, to share their artwork. I have two images published in this book. I'm amazed at the company I'm keeping: artists from every media sharing their hearts for God and how God is speaking to them through art. It's exciting to be a part of this adventure and book! — Becky Davis, *Fine Arts Photographer*

Dedication

This book is dedicated to Carmen Vera-Shababy, Zahava Raz, Shirley Mize and the many other prophetic artists who allow the truth of God's love to shine through their work.

Acknowledgements

Many thanks to all the artists who allowed their stories, art and advice to be part of this book. They are listed in order by their first names: Alex Radin, Amelia Whaley, Audrey Pryst, Barbara Velez, Becky Jane Davis, Brad Ferguson, Brenda Tarasenko, Brian Russelburg, Carmen Vera-Shababy, Cathie Zurek-Geske, Charlene Mueller, Christine Cole, Dale Baker, Dale Olsen, Diana Estes, Donna Lehrer, Evan Okpisz, Gail Simons, Gelene Keever, Gwendolyn S. Fullenwider, Jacqueline Martorano, Janet Hart Heinicke, Justice Carmon, Lyn Rowley, Marianne Chen, Mary Sheesley-Warburton, Matt Lawlor, Matt Tommey, Mitzi Blanchard, Natalie Lombard, Natalie Totire, Paula MinGucci, Peggy Wilmeth Carr, Phillip W. Hoagland, Rachael Weidman, Risa Baldauf, Rosalinda V. Lopez, Rose Calkins, Rosie Martindale, Ruth LaSure, Shirley Mize, Steve Nelson, Suja Jacob, Susan Zimmer, Tim Botts, Tricia Rush, Trisha L. Stern, and Zahava Raz.

Many thanks to Bob Hay, Executive Director of Karitos Christian Art Confereneces, for writing the foreword. Bob is an amazing person who follows the amazing visions God gives him.

Many thanks to novelist Paul R. Lloyd for editing and proofreading.

A special thank you to Ellen Huxtable for our early morning meetings, for helping me with the book title, for walking alongside me through this amazing journey of discovery, and for praying with me.

Many thanks to the prayer warriors: Carmen Vera-Shababy, Jeannette Kielp, Justice Carmon, Michele Cambric, Peggy Carr, Rich and Kay Fick, Theresa Phillips and Zahava Raz. And a big thank you to my small group: Dawn and Steve Okpisz, Diane Olson, Jane Rakow, Kathy Ragsdale and Lillian Kutz. Your prayers strengthened, sustained and enabled me to move forward despite obstacles and delays.

Highest thanks and praise to Jesus Christ, my Lord and Savior, who placed the idea for this book on my heart, and then opened the hearts of artists to be part of it. It's His power, His strength, His enablement and His guidance that made this book possible.

Also, many thanks to the team of volunteers who make the Karitos Christian Arts Conference a reality. It was through Karitos, that I had the privilege of taking workshops, teaching classes, serving on the steering committee, and even one year, serving as the Visual Arts Department Head. Being part of Karitos helped me grow and step out in my calling as a prophetic artist, author, and speaker.

Foreword by Bob Hay, Executive Director of Karitos

I was excited when Lynn asked me to write the foreword for this book. You see, the day before she called, a woman who had attended the Karitos Christian Arts Conference called and was telling me that Lynn had become a mentor to her. As a result, God was now touching lives in amazing ways through this woman's art.

Prophetic art is a relatively new form of ministry, and Lynn has been one of its leading proponents. Now, with the release of this book, she introduces us to fifty prophetic artists, including herself. Not only do we see samples of their work, but each one shares a word of advice for the readers. *Speaking to the Heart* will be a valuable resource for those wanting to go deeper in their understanding of prophetic art.

Allow me to share a story from Karitos 2007. This was a watershed year for Karitos in regards to prophetic ministry, and especially prophetic art. Vivien Hibbert was with us for the first time. Her book, *Prophetic Worship*, is considered by many to be the finest ever written on the subject. On Saturday afternoon, she brought a variety of artists together in a 90-minute teaching/demonstration on prophetic worship. To quote Vivien:

> "Singers are the keepers
>   of the words of God.
> Musicians are the keepers
>   of the sounds of God.
> Dancers and all visual artists
>   are keepers of the sight of God.
> Every artist is a keeper
>   of the fragrance of God!"

The prophetic would be powerfully manifested later that evening. It began with art — Prophetic Art! Vivien took the microphone to call our attention to a large painting that was nearing completion on the stage. The painting depicted the prophet Isaiah looking heavenward as a pair of tongs with a burning coal was about to touch his lips. As we gazed upon the painting, the worship team began to play, "*I See the Lord*" — a song taken from Isaiah, chapter six. The worship list had been prepared several months earlier, with no knowledge of the painting.

The song had a powerful impact on the audience and many were at the altar as it came to a close. The song ended, but the prophetic continued. A hush spread across the auditorium as the worship leader began to blow quietly into the microphone; the sound was like a gentle wind. The Holy Spirit began to move in different ways — in song, dance, flags, banners, and even a Jericho March.

Twenty to thirty minutes later, two of our leaders came to the stage with tears in their eyes, to announce that a beloved member of our faculty had just received word that her father had stopped breathing. She and her children were en route to the hospital.

Two worship team members began a call and response. Sitting on stage was a second large painting that the artist had done the previous evening. It showed a woman sitting curled up "shielded with His wings, sheltered with His feathers" as the Psalmist has said. Someone picked up the painting and began to slowly raise it up and down in a wing-like fashion. The words coming from the worship team were at first words of solace, then peace, comfort, hope and at the last, joy.

This was one of the most memorable Karitos evenings we've ever had. I share it here not simply to illustrate the power of prophetic art, but to encourage you as an artist. While you may not paint before crowds of people, know that your gift — when placed in God's hands — can have the same dramatic impact, even if only shared with a lost friend or a grieving loved one.

— *Bob Hay,*
Executive Director of Karitos
Christian Art Conferences
www.karitos.com

Welcome

Today is the day the Lord raises up His prophetic visual artists. He calls forth the young and the old, the skilled and those who are just beginning to step out and make visual representations of HIS love and the messages HE conveys.

This book is created to glorify the Lord, to show what HE is doing through HIS artists, to encourage those being called into the area of prophetic visual art, and to become a resource for artists, teachers, pastors, churches and people who want to know more about prophetic art. It is also a book people can use to connect with other prophetic artists, especially for prayer and support.

All of God's artists are precious to Jesus Christ. Their work is a blessing to Him and to the people they touch. And so are the stories that go with the art.

Prophetic artist Carmen Vera-Shababy paints on stage at one of the Karitos Christian Arts Conferences.

Scripture and Art

When we delve into Scripture for wisdom, the Holy Spirit gives us insight. The book of Genesis explains that our creative God made the universe, and what HE created was good. Because we are made in HIS image, we are also creative — particularly HIS artists. Therefore, when we paint or make art using ideas that the Lord gives us, it is good.

1 Corinthians 12:7-10 talks about the Holy Spirit giving spiritual gifts for the common good. These gifts include wisdom, knowledge, faith, healing, miraculous powers, prophecy and more. When an artist is given these gifts, he/she is also able to draw or paint what God gives to convey HIS wisdom, knowledge, healing and messages in a visual manner.

1 Timothy 4:14 warns not to neglect our gift. Art is a gift. And when the Lord impresses upon us to create a picture HE places in our minds, we need to do it.

God gives HIS people visions. Ezekiel 1:1-28 and Ezekiel 8:3 describe visions God gave Ezekiel. In Daniel, chapters 7, 8, 9, and 10, the Lord gives various visions to Daniel, and in Zechariah 1:8-21, the Lord gives a vision to Zechariah. Over the years, artists have sketched, painted and illustrated visions that were recorded in the Bible.

In the New Testament, the Lord gave Zechariah a vision in Luke 1:21-22, HE gave Peter a vision in Acts 10:9-16, and Paul a vision in Acts 16:9. The Holy Spirit gave John a vision of Christ in Revelation 1:12-16. We try to picture these visions in our head, but an artist who receives visions from the Lord is able to sketch them on paper.

In Numbers 21:8-9, God asked Moses to make a sculpture — an image of a snake on a pole. After he made it, God used this piece of art to heal people who repented and looked at it. God heals people today through art, when they see a painting or sculpture that draws them into repentance.

Joel 2:28 and Acts 2:17 talk about the Lord pouring out His Spirit on all people in the last days — that our sons and daughters will prophesy, old men will dream dreams, and young men will see visions. Many artists are receiving dreams and visions today. And they are putting what they see into paintings, drawings and other forms of art.

Numbers 31:50-52 talks about Moses and Eleazar the priest accepting gold — all the crafted articles — from the commanders of the Israelites. Crafted articles are a form of art. And God accepts our art that is offered to HIM when we create what HE impresses upon us.

Joshua 6:19 talks about all the silver, gold and articles of bronze and iron being sacred to the Lord, and must be brought into HIS treasury. These articles would have included decorative art pieces. The art we create is sacred to God, too. Our art belongs in the Lord's treasury — to be used by HIM anyway HE wants it used.

2 Samuel 8:9-11 talks about Tou, King of Hamath bringing King David articles of silver, gold and bronze, and King David dedicating these articles to the Lord. Our art needs to be dedicated to the Lord.

In 2 Chronicles 2:7, King Solomon called for skilled artists to work on building and decorating the sanctuary of the Lord. "Send me, therefore, a man skilled to work in gold and silver, bronze and iron, and in purple, crimson and blue yarn, and experienced in the art of engraving, to work in Judah and Jerusalem with my skilled workers, whom my father David provided." We need to become skilled artists and craftsmen.

Exodus 31:1-5 shows that God can fill artists with wisdom, knowledge and understanding. "Then the LORD said to Moses, "See, I have chosen Bezalel son of Uri, the son of Hur, of the tribe of Judah, and I have filled him with the Spirit of God, with wisdom, with understanding, with knowledge and with all kinds of skills — to make artistic designs for work in gold, silver and bronze, to cut and set stones, to work in wood, and to engage in all kinds of crafts."

All kinds of artist were needed to build the Tabernacle, which was a replica of the heavenly vision God showed Moses. Exodus 35:23 and 35:25-27 says, "Everyone who had blue, purple or scarlet yarn or fine linen, or goat hair, ram skins dyed red or the other durable leather brought them ... Every skilled woman spun with her hands and brought what she had spun — blue, purple or scarlet yarn or fine linen. And all the women who were willing and had the skill spun the goat hair. The leaders brought onyx stones and other gems to be mounted on the ephod and breastpiece." If the body of Christ makes resources available to its artists, then artists can create art that the Lord calls forth to strengthen the body of believers.

Exodus 26:1 shows that fabric art has been honored as a form of art since ancient times. "Make the tabernacle with ten curtains of finely twisted linen and blue, purple and scarlet yarn, with cherubim woven into them by a skilled worker."

Exodus 35:10 calls artists to step forward. "All who are skilled among you are to come and make everything the LORD has commanded." Today, the Lord calls HIS artists to step forward and create art that HE commands. When God tells us to create art from the pictures HE places in our head, it's called prophetic art because HE speaks it into our hearts just as HE spoke with prophets in the Old Testament and with disciples in the New Testament.

Exodus 35:35 shows that it is God who fills HIS artists with skill. "He has filled them with skill to do all kinds of work as engravers, designers, embroiderers in blue, purple and scarlet yarn and fine linen, and weavers — all of them skilled workers and designers."

Song of Songs 7:1 shows that art is treasured, "How beautiful your sandaled feet, O prince's daughter! Your graceful legs are like jewels, the work of an artist's hands." As artists, we are to produce art that can be treasured. And what a treasure it is to create art that the Lord uses to speak into people's hearts.

Proverbs 22:29 says, "Do you see those who are skilled in their work? They will serve before kings; they will not serve before officials of low rank." As we hone our artistic skills and offer our talents to Yahweh, we will serve before the King of kings — the Lord Jesus Christ.

1 Thessalonians 5:19-20 warns us, "Do not put out the Spirit's fire; do not treat prophecies with contempt." When the Lord tells an artist to make a certain picture and the artist obeys, it becomes prophetic and should never be treated with contempt.

I Corinthians 14:3 says, "But those who prophesy speak to people for their strengthening, encouraging and comfort." If the Lord is using art to strengthen, encourage and comfort, don't fight it. God is sovereign. Let HIM do what HE wants to do, in whatever manner HE wants to do it in, and that includes art.

1 Corinthians chapter 12 shows us that gifts operate within the body of Christ. Christian prophetic art cannot be independent of the body of Christ. Prophetic art must agree with Scriptural promises, exalt the Lord, bless/benefit the followers of Jesus, and be in community — for we are not called to live life alone.

As artists rise up in using their talents as the Lord directs, churches need to honor their artistic members as they step into creating prophetic art. For the Lord is doing marvelous things.

Why I wrote this book

Over the past five years, the Lord has been, and continues to, place prophetic artists into my life. Many are boldly walking in their calling. These artists overflow with joy and exuberance. I love meeting them and seeing what they create. Their art causes a greater awareness of the splendor, love and compassion of Jesus Christ, to rise up from within my heart.

Other talented, prophetic artists have barriers and roadblocks in their lives — hurts, wounds, discouragement or rejection that keeps them from fully walking in their calling. Some have friends or family who can't grasp the fact that God uses artists. Others are limited by church leadership. All of them need encouragement and opportunities to grow and hear more from the Lord.

The Holy Spirit placed compassion in my heart for struggling prophetic artists, because I struggle, too. He prompted me to walk with and beside other artists, to encourage them, to share what HE has been teaching me about stepping out in faith despite fear, and to show them how to enjoy the freedom Christ gives us to create art with HIM.

So when the Holy Spirit put the idea on my heart to create a book showing how widely Jesus Christ speaks to people's hearts through art today, and to invite all types of visual artists, who work in all kinds of media, who have diverse ethnic backgrounds, are different ages, and live in various parts of North America, to be part of this book, I jumped for joy.

Journeying with Jesus, as one of His artist/writers, and learning to step into the picture HE paints each day, has been, and continues to be, an awesome experience. I love being a prophetic artist because it's all about HIM — Jesus Christ — who sets us free to be who HE calls us to be! For once I was lost, but now I am found!

May you enjoy and be blessed by this book as much as, or even more than, I was in putting it together.

LOST AND FOUND

Lynn Zuk-Lloyd

What is prophetic art?

Prophetic art is art that the Lord uses to speak to people's hearts. It's a picture Christ works through to blanket His love around us, or a painting He draws us into to comfort our aching souls. It's a tool HE uses to unlock hearts so we can receive wisdom and understanding. It's a door the Holy Spirit opens to usher us into the miraculous — into the supernatural — so we can have a spiritual encounter with Jesus Christ.

The Holy Spirit uses art to trigger the innermost part of our being, so we can respond, receive and be blessed by Yahweh — the Lord God Most High. God shows us through art, how deeply HE cares about us. HE stirs the longings of our heart through pictures and uses illustrations as a venue for HIM to minister into those deep, dark, secret, places where no one else can enter.

Thus, prophetic art becomes a visual opportunity to receive hope, truth and healing as the Holy Spirit illuminates, enlightens and awakens us to Christ's all-encompassing, all-powerful, compassionate love.

Let us celebrate the increase of prophetic art in today's world. For all of us need encouragement, refreshing, strengthening and renewal. And if the Lord wants to use art as a means to minister to HIS people, let us embrace what He is doing!

Copyright © 2012 Zahava Raz. Used with permission.

Prophetic portrait artist, Zahava Raz, captures the awe and wonder of an angel looking towards the Lord. She was experimenting with a simple art program on her computer and this was the result. Her gentle drawings that she emailed to friends, have touched many people with hope, joy and assurance of God's love.

What is the difference between a prophetic act and prophetic art?

A prophetic "ACT" is when the Lord tells a person to do something, and the person complies. A prophetic act is the response of the artist to the Holy Spirit's request to draw a picture and give it to someone, or to paint at a Christian gathering. Prophetic "ART" is the result of the artist's obedience.

It's important not to confuse a prophetic act with prophetic art. The Holy Spirit can use art we create or a photograph we take, even if we aren't keenly aware of Him telling us to do so. HE can use art we experiment with, or a sketch we compose just for the sheer joy of drawing something, if HE wants to.

So please don't get hung up on whether or not a piece of art is prophetic based on HIM talking to you about it before or after you create it.

Instead, focus on growing your relationship with Jesus Christ and practicing your listening skills so you can hear Him better. Grow in strengthening and developing your talent, while releasing your art, who you are, and what you do, to the Lord. Then relax! Let God work out the details as you have fun delighting yourself in HIM and in creating art. For the joy of the Lord is your strength, and the Holy Spirit will guide you.

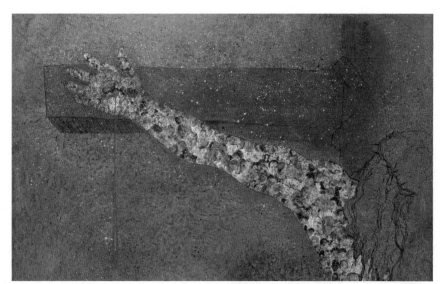

This amazing piece of art became reality, because Mitzi Blanchard stepped out in a prophetic act of obedience to create a prophetic piece of art. A larger picture of this art can be seen on page 45.

How is prophetic art created?

Creating prophetic art is an expression of love and obedience that springs from a relationship between the Creator and HIS artist. Receiving revelation about a piece of art can happen before, during or even after the art is created.

The Holy Spirit can deposit a complete picture into the artist's mind, or reveal a few elements HE wants the artist to work with. The Lord might instruct the artist to reproduce the picture exactly as he sees it, or use the image as a starting point. God might bring a Scripture, teaching or event to the artist's mind to illustrate.

Sometimes the Holy Spirit prompts the artist to start drawing or sculpting first — to be free to just place the brush or pencil on paper and let the art emerge with no preconceived idea of what it will look like. It's like a dance with the Lord. HE leads and we follow.

Other times, the Lord will show the artist exactly what materials to use, what style to work in, what colors to choose, and what size to make the art. HE even shops with the artist to find the supplies to make the art, if we invite HIM.

One of the amazing things that's beginning to happen at conferences and worship services is the Lord enabling HIS artists to create art in "real time." An artist may start with an idea prompted by the Lord, but as the Holy Spirit moves, the artist finds himself painting what the Lord is doing as it happens!

Jesus enjoys HIS artists and has fun working with them. The Holy Spirit even likes to hide things and watch HIS artists discover HIS Hand at work in their art.

How exciting it is to find hidden images in our painting that the Lord placed there!

Or to come to the realization that the Holy Spirit is not only guiding us, but also drawing with us!

God not only calls HIS artists to follow HIS leading in creating a particular piece of art, but to also play, explore, experiment and hone our skills. For out of "play" comes enjoyment. Out of enjoyment comes revelation. And out of revelation comes wisdom and understanding.

Each artist is different, and the Lord speaks to each one of us in unique ways. These ways can be subtle or jolting, eye-opening or thought provoking, enlightening and filled with insight, or totally outlandish!

And then there are times when the artist doesn't even know that a piece of art created years earlier, or a photograph taken just for fun, had prophetic meaning until the Lord speaks into his or her heart. And sometimes HE will use a piece of our art we don't even like!

As prophetic artists, it's important to grow our faith and fine tune our skills. This takes practice on our part, but is necessary because people need to be touched not only by the Holy Spirit working through our art, but also by the beauty of what we create. Because God is excellent at everything HE does, we need to become excellent in the work we do.

And as we diligently work at developing and honing our skills, the Holy Spirit lovingly works at turning ordinary artists into master craftsmen.

For the power behind prophetic art is never the artist, but Jesus Christ, Himself, who calls the invisible to become visible, and the imaginative to become real.

How is prophetic art used?

The most common way prophetic art is used is to worship the Lord. This is when artists offer their talents with joy, thanksgiving, celebration and praise. They exalt Christ by drawing, painting, or making what the Holy Spirit places in their hearts.

The most noticeable form of prophetic art is prophetic performance art. This is when the artist creates, paints, sculpts or draws on stage during worship to convey what the Lord is doing, or to illustrate the message the Holy Spirit wants the audience to receive.

Message art is another way prophetic art is used. This happens when the Lord gives the artist a message to illustrate and then instructs the artist to either give or show the art to a specific person or a group of people. The art may even contain different messages for different people.

Prophetic art is also used to bring about emotional and spiritual healing, either to the person who is making the art, or through a piece of art the Lord instructs an artist to make that is given to, or seen by, someone else. Art by itself does not heal. The Holy Spirit uses art as a tool to bring someone more fully into health and wholeness.

Workshops, artist gatherings and conferences can be places where prophetic art is created and used. As the workshop leader seeks the Lord, God gives him/her a theme, Scripture, or message HE wants participants to receive. Then art is created as the Holy Spirit inspires and directs.

Small group settings are great places to discover how the Lord not only speaks to the individual, but also strengthens the entire group as artists "show and tell."

How can prophetic art become more visible?

Prophetic artists have the responsibility to get their art into places where people can benefit from seeing it, as the Lord directs. These places might include exhibits or displays at galleries, churches, conferences, fairs and other events. Or they might include printed materials, such as books, cards, art prints, posters, and flyers that can be distributed to a wider audience.

Some prophetic artists feel a holy nudge to include their art in the newsletters, blogs and videos they create, or to show their work on their website. Other artists feel prompted to take their paintings and speak to every group willing to hear God's message of love. And some artists are guided by the Holy Spirit to create a piece of art for just one person or one ministry, and they are blessed as they step out and do this.

Social media is another venue that makes prophetic art more visible. It's a great place to show, share and sell art. It's also an exciting way to find other prophetic artists and art groups to connect with or become part of.

Community is a huge factor for prophetic artists. We are not called to walk alone, but to gather, support, encourage and minister to each other.

For artists who also speak, the Lord might instruct the person to give away a piece of art prophetically. The first time this happened to me, fear seized my heart. What if no one in the audience wanted the art? What if people thought I was crazy? After many "what if's" I finally told the Lord I would obey HIM, but there needed to be someone eager to receive each art print. There was!

The secret to using prophetic art and making it more visible is to always do it God's way. When HE invites you to paint in a park, at a zoo or at an outdoor event, do it. When HE prompts you to sketch in the pew, then sketch. When HE tells you to paint in front of other people during worship, step forth boldly. When HE says to give art prints or a painting away, give them as directed. When HE nudges you to sell your art, sell it. When HE asks you to teach, speak or lead prophetic art workshops, go for it. Whatever the Lord leads you to do, jump in with joy and excitement, trusting HIM to be with you, helping you, every step of the way.

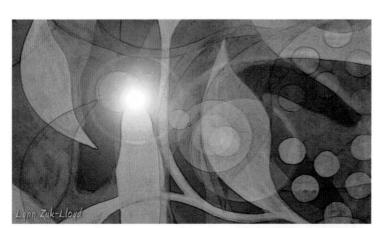

The Lord encourages Lynn Zuk-Lloyd to create prophetic art to use in her email newsletters.

What else do people need to know about prophetic art?

Prophetic art is important, and being an artist for the Lord is a high calling. God uses visual art to speak to the dark hidden, secret places within the heart that are held in bondage, consumed by pain, racked with discouragement, or gripped with disappointment. These are walled-in places where words cannot penetrate. But art can.

Unfortunately, misunderstandings have developed in the church and among Christians about what prophetic art is or is not, how it should or should not be used, and how it needs to be created. With the rise of more and more prophetic artists, it's important to understand the purpose and nature of Christian prophetic art. It's vital to know that the Lord brings hope, healing and reconciliation through the work of His artists.

Also know that when God speaks to the artist about a piece of art after it was created, does not make it less prophetic than if the Lord had given clear instructions up front. What makes art prophetic is not when it was made, but the fact that the Lord uses the art to speak to someone's heart.

What does prophetic art look like?

Prophetic art takes on many shapes and forms. It can be produced in any medium, any style and any size that best shows the message the Lord wants to convey. The art can be simple or intricate, and created with any type of tool or material.

Be careful not to judge what prophetic art is or is not. The art you see, or the art you create, may not speak to you personally. But it may bring someone else to their knees in tears, or cause them to leap with joy and thanksgiving at what the Lord spoke into their heart.

Also, do not judge the quality of a piece of prophetic art, or criticize the tool it was created with. David used a slingshot to slay Goliath. A childlike drawing sketched with a crayon can be just as powerful as David's slingshot.

The following pages contain many types of prophetic art by artists of varying backgrounds and abilities, from beginners to established artists with professional careers.

Many of these artists also dance, sing, write, compose and speak. Others have a single focus — visual art. All are important. All are dedicated to the Lord, offering their talents to Jesus Christ. All are commissioned by the God to illustrate truth.

Truth brings us into the Light, so that it may be plainly seen that what we have done, we have done through God. (Based on John 3:21)

God the Father calls His artists into action.

Title: It's Time to Paint
Medium: Acrylic
Artist: Diana Estes

I have been in a season of learning who I am in the Lord and my place in His Kingdom. I think we will never stop learning as long as we walk with Him, but this season has been especially important to me because I have been stepping out more in the gifts that He has given me, and sharing them with others. I have learned that the journey itself is our story of His grace, and that everything we go through, wonderful and tough, will always find its way in His hands to be used for our growth and restoration.

It was around this time that God showed me the vision of His right arm being stretched out before me. Behind His arm was the entire universe, including the planet earth. In His hand was a pocket watch with the time 5:55 on it. This number was incredibly significant to me because this was connected to a promise made to me several years earlier. It was related to a prophecy over my life and my first prophetic painting that had been confirmed by other prophets. It is also a number that represents grace and the powerful tools we have access to through His grace. I also saw a key in His hand. I believe that He was telling me that the things that had been stolen from us were not lost but that He held the key to everything and the release of the promises in our lives. As I began to paint what I saw, I was not able to paint the key in His hand, but I began to see a paint brush instead. Later, I would come to realize that the paintbrush was the key to unlocking these promises in my life in this season. It was His will for me to paint for His glory and His will for many others as well.

It was not too long after this that I would learn from many other artists that they were also feeling a call to rise up during this season and share with others what God was speaking through their art. That each of our art forms are our tools of spiritual warfare. God uses restoration paint, and He has been restoring those chosen for this task in the body to also be restorers. These artist are being used by the Lord to bring a unique perspective of God's heart to each of us, including the lost.

Biography

My name is Diana Estes. I live in a small town, Aurora, Missouri, with my husband and best friend, Chad Estes and our youngest daughter. I love being a wife, mother, and grandma.

I grew up being blessed to have a very artistic grandmother that has always encouraged art in my life. So art has been a part of my life for as long as I can remember. I had begun moving in prophetic art several years ago, beginning with my own prophecy as my first prophetic piece.

Since then, I have grown increasingly comfortable painting for God in whatever He chooses to give me or inspire me with. Painting is very much a part of my relationship with the Lord. I consider it a great privilege to be led by the Holy Spirit to co-create with my Heavenly Father.

Our family also enjoys the love and invaluable support we receive from our church family, Summit Revival Center, in Aurora, Missouri.

Contact Information

Email: artsydiana555@gmail.com   Blog: TheHealingLeaves.blogspot.com

Advice

My advice to every artist wanting to move in the prophetic is to seek the face of Jesus. When you begin to desire more intimacy with the Lord, you will find yourself being spoken to on a more intimate level. This will include every area of your life, especially those areas where you are most gifted by God.

I found that my walk with Him in my art is a learning experience for me in every season of my life. You may be expressing something for others about God's heart that they haven't experienced before, but you will also be in the process of learning and exploring God's heart for yourself. There may even be times that your journey is a little painful — when pruning is necessary by God to bring about Godly character. But those will be very powerful expressions for your life, as well as others.

Prophecy doesn't always come to me at once. Sometimes He gives me pieces that end up fitting together perfectly and completing the picture. Be obedient to the Spirit, and let the prophecy work itself out in God's time.

The Lord has a purpose for our art.

Title: A Call to Purpose
Medium: Acrylic on canvas
Artist: Charlene Mueller

Copyright © 2011 Charlene Mueller. Used with permission.

One morning, during a pause in the worship, a deacon of my church was moved by the Holy Spirit to speak to us. He shared the vision of our church as an embattled ship, sails full in the wind, and a cross emblazoned on the mainsail. It steers through angry waters amid threats of disaster, driven on its rescue mission by Christ's love for a sea of lost souls. As he spoke, his words became alive in my mind. I went home and started to paint.

The clipper ship represents the Church of Jesus Christ — each church, perhaps, its own ship — or the ship as Christ's Church, entire. All the people on board are dressed in white, a sign that they belong to Jesus. The ship is surrounded by a violent storm; waves swelling high lift the ship, and then heaves it low. Rising from the sea, a terrible serpent heads for the ship's bow—waiting for the opportunity to strike … the enemy never sleeps. The longboats are hard-pressed to reach the ship as the waves of the world vie for the souls of men.

There is, however, a protective calm directly around the ship. The Father is watching over the rescuers, His guiding light shining down through a bright tear in the wind-tossed sky. Two of the longboats reach the ship; rope ladders drop over the railing, and hails go out to encourage the exhausted survivors.

In the remaining longboats, the reactions vary. There is a family in one boat. The husband bravely stands, waving his kerchief and pleading through the wind, "Rescue us!" Others, sit crouched in fear; they will have to be snatched from peril by a willing soul, someone who will risk his or her own life to climb over the railing and down a moving ladder to grab hold of them. In another boat, there are those who ignore the hope extended; they are listening only to the lies told by their pride-shaped hearts. Each voices the same reply, "I don't need You!" Jesus, even now, bids them to come.

Sadly, in the corner, the waves seem to have captured an empty longboat. As I look, my heart feels heavy — and empty at the same time. I sink below the waters with it. This boat represents the lost. Who were these people? Was there no one to help them? Its emptiness is as profound as eternity.

Charlene Mueller has compiled her prophetic paintings into a book. Painting by painting, experience by experience, you will discover the ability God gave her to communicate in paint and the written word. Jesus working in the lives of people, eagles, soap, mice, and a mountain are a small sampling of the images captured in Charlene's book.

Painting with God is available on Amazon.com or through Ajoyin Publishing, www.ajoyin.com

Jesus assures us He is with us.

Title: Jesus Walking Through the Woods
Medium: Acrylic on canvas
Artist: Charlene Mueller

This was painted in the spot where campers would have a bonfire, and sit around and talk. It was a place where they would roast marshmallows and have Bible Study. Because it was a Christian campground, the whole of the grounds had HIS PRESENCE filling it. Everywhere, everywhere you walked was holy ground. As I walked in the woods, the Holy Spirit would answer SO many questions.

One day, I walked the woods and set up my easel. I felt Jesus' presence and painted very fast. I like painting fast! If you look closely at the painting, you will notice that Jesus is painted in Spirit — with no feet touching the ground.

Biography

Charlene Mueller, mother of two, grandmother to six, is a past president of an Aglow International Lighthouse, serving ten years. She attends Maranatha Assembly of God Church in McHenry, Illinois. She has garnered a few nicknames over her life, including Sparkplug and Pit Bull, (a funny story for another time), but the one she lights up to is Encourager, as this is her heart.

Contact Information

Email: PaintingwithGod@muellernetwork.com

Advice

To be a fisher of men — to keep His truth and, as He leads, to offer salvation; this is the greatest of privileges. My own rod, reel, and bait are made of words, paint and paintbrushes. At this very moment, men and women the world over are on their knees, fashioning fishing flies of prayer. This prayer will be a covering for those who have put on wading boots and are going out into the deep waters of life. In heaven, there is a storehouse filled with fishing rods of hope, nets of kindness, and tackle boxes filled with love. Jesus is tending the pick-up window today. Your fishing gear is ready. It is just a prayer away.

Through Christ, we ascend to the throne of grace.

Title: Out of the Grey
Medium: Acrylic on Birch Wood Panel
Artist: Alex Radin

This piece "Out of the Grey" is about walking in God's power, out of a mediocre life into the land of color and vibrancy. It is an encouragement to trust and surrender completely to the Lord and be charged up with everything He has for us.

As I was painting this piece during a conference at a church in Charleston, South Carolina, it began to snow (which only happens there about once every ten years), and the power was lost in the building for several minutes. Then it came back on. It was a tangible sign to all of us at the conference that the Lord was speaking: if we trust in man's power, it may fail us, but through His power we will be conveyed from the land of grey to the land of color and light.

Biography

Alex Radin is primarily a painter working in oils and acrylics. He attended the Columbus College of Art and Design in Columbus, Ohio and graduated with a BFA. His work has shown in both solo and group exhibitions in Ohio, South Carolina, North Carolina, Illinois, and Texas.

Alex burns with a passion to intersect culture and reach people with God's love and power. He is driven to help other artists hear the voice of God and create from a place of intimacy with Christ. He has traveled nationally encouraging and training artists and is co-founder of an arts organization, "Artist on Fire," along with his wife Sara.

Alex Radin was the Visual Arts Department Head for the 2013 Karitos Christian Art Conference.

Contact Information

Website: www.truthillustrations.com

Artist On Fire
Website: artistonfire.com
Email: info@artistonfire.com

Advice

Seek to grow in deep intimacy with the Lord. Ask Him to grow you in your artistic gifting. Seek to offer Him your very best. Continually seek to grow in your technical ability. Create what you are passionate about.

Yahweh understands the intricacies of life.

Title: Sons & Daughters
Medium: Basketry
Retail price: $2,500
Artist: Matt Tommey

Matt Tommey

My basketry work is a collaboration between me, the inspiration of the Holy Spirit and the natural materials I use. Rarely do I ever come to a piece with specific prophetic content in mind. However, almost always once the piece is completed, it begins to speak to me and to the viewer in a prophetic manner, drawing us closer to the purposes of God in our own lives.

This piece in particular, called "Sons and Daughters," is a part of a series I'm currently in, focusing on the nature of community, relationship and the dynamics of living among others in the context of the Kingdom. It is three bark and vine baskets nested in laurel branches and colored with black walnut dye.

This beautiful piece of art sold at Arrowmont School of Arts and Crafts while being featured in the National Basketry Organization, Inc. 7th Biennial Exhibition, "All Things Considered VII." It traveled to the Fuller Craft Museum in Boston and then on to live permanently in San Francisco, California.

Biography

Matt Tommey has been a basketry artist for over 20 years, working primarily in the weaving of locally available bark, vines and recycled metal into sculptural containers and forms. Matt is a leader in the contemporary basketry movement, serving on the Board of Directors of the National Basketry Organization and as an instructor at schools, guilds and conventions around the country including Arrowmont School of Arts & Crafts and the John C. Campbell Folk School.

In 2009, Matt founded The Worship Studio (www.theworshipstudio.org) an international arts ministry that helps artists around the world reveal the Glory of God through their creative expression. He is also an author, a popular conference speaker, and a worship leader.

Contact Information

Website: www.matttommey.com
Email: matt@matttommey.com

Advice

I believe all creativity has the capacity to be prophetic because all creativity carries light and life — the very nature — of God in and through it. When God reveals Himself to man, no matter the form, transformation is always the result.

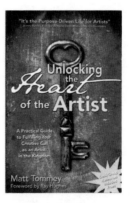 

Matt Tommey wrote two amazing books:

Unlocking the Heart of the Artist gives artists depth and understanding to the call on their lives, shows the importance of unleashing the creative talent God gave them, and explains the power of placing their identity in Jesus Christ.

Crafting Your Brand offers excellent advice on marketing and branding art. Both books are available on Amazon.com

Truth dispels darkness.

Title: Truth Banner
Medium: Textile art
Artist: Natalie Lombard

The original TRUTH BANNER was my thank you to a lawyer who helped me gratis on a difficult project. An obvious visual for a banner for a lawyer's office was the statue of Lady Justice. As I prayed, another image came, of the battle leading to justice: the battle over truth. The lawyer gratefully received the 7 foot by 11 foot banner, regal in royal blue velvet background.

In the 1990's, there was an ongoing battle in our nation, the existence of Truth itself, as challenged by relativism. I re-created the TRUTH BANNER using a shimmering turquoise fabric for background, intensifying the contrast between light and darkness. Years before I created either banner, the Lord told me to buy this fabric, the last sixteen yards of it on the bolt, at a price I normally could not afford. I usually did not buy huge quantities without an art commission, so I asked the Lord for confirmation. He told me I would need the fabric one distant day.

I sought to hang the second Truth Banner where leaders in the Congress and Senate of our country cast their votes. But no philosophical art of any kind is allowed in the Federal voting chambers nor along the corridors leading to those chambers, and likewise not in any of the state capitols' voting chambers and corridors.

The banner next hung at Church of the Resurrection in West Chicago. One youth, after pondering the determined countenance of the massive angel, was inspired to take a stand for God's truth at his school where police routinely dealt with gang-related violence. One man felt convicted for his deceptive business dealings by the dark fabrics slithering up to extinguish the word TRUTH. One child decided to trust Jesus amidst his fears living in an abusive and chaotic home.

The banner currently is on loan at Cyrus Ministries International in Big Rock, Illinois, where people from all over the world come to study God's Word and to pray. With God's grace, may they become the next leaders in God's plan for this fallen world.

Biography
I pursued art in various media, as a college teacher of oral interpretation, as an actress in New York City, and as a fashion designer, each of which prepared me for creating large worship banners for churches.

Contact Information
Website: www.splendorinworship.com

Advice
There is a temptation to create spectacle. Instead, choose splendor. Balance your need to make a living with what you long to say or contribute to our world, but persistently pursue God's Kingdom.

My slogan for my banner business was, "To gladden the heart, to nourish the mind, to enrich the soul through invigorating and thought-provoking art." What's yours?

"A man was healed as we prayed for him at Cyrus Ministries International. We celebrated in front of the truth banner!" — Rich Fick

The radiance of Christ's love leads us towards victory.

Title: The Victory Cross
Medium: Textile art
Artist: Natalie Lombard

One year during Lent, when many Christians purposely focus on Christ's suffering for us on the cross, I ardently did not want to focus there, even though He willingly died to pay for the sins of all human beings. Rather, I wanted to thank Him every moment of the days and nights leading up to Easter, and then celebrate His Victory over sin and death.

Traditionally artists have depicted the cross as an instrument of torture, for so it was. Traditionally artists have depicted it as splintery wood to which Jesus was nailed. Many artists have emphasized the amount of blood that may have poured from his wounds, an emphasis which often is gruesome, shocking, in all trying to get the viewer to feel compassion, nay, empathy, no, not that either, but to grasp at some level the horrendous guilt of human beings for their sin against God and His Creation.

But this particular Lent, I just couldn't ponder any longer these ugly realities about Jesus's huge substitutionary death for us. I wanted to point myself toward what Scripture describes as "the joy set before Him."

Church of the Resurrection, in West Chicago, Illinois, has a splintery wooden cross, 18 feet tall and a crossbar of 8 feet. I wrapped it entirely in pure white brocade. Long ripples of gold lamé emanated from the center, upwards and outward left and right far beyond the cross. A huge bouquet of white gladiolas and golden fronds was affixed onto the cross's permanent crown of thorns, covering it completely from view, with golden ribbons cascading from this crown of flowers.

Easter Vigil is held the night before Easter Sunday. It starts entirely in darkness. The Paschal candle was carried into the sanctuary. Its flame was distributed to the smaller candles held by each parishioner. A soft glow filled the sanctuary. At one moment in the service all the electrical lights were turned on at once, everyone shouted "Alleluia!" and we all rang bells each had brought from home. There in front of us stood the Victory Cross of our Savior! Gleaming white and gold, radiating throughout the sanctuary, ablaze with Light.

The next day, after the Easter service, a man told me privately that he had ruined his marriage by his addiction to pornography. He had tried to stop many times but felt overwhelmed by its power. He had ridiculed people who talked about the benefits of living pure, and sneered at the concept of purity itself. But as he gazed at the pure white cross, he saw for the first time in his life the utter splendor of purity, a splendor that made him want to hide, at the same time riveting his eyes to what he now saw as exquisite, humble, victorious purity. He got professional help and did indeed clean his house of pornography.

Natalie Lombard has written and created a book about banners to share her expertise and wisdom on banner making. *Splendor in Worship* is filled with knowledge, insight and photos of her huge variety of banners, plus instructions on how you can make excellent banners yourself. Her book will soon be available to the public. To pre-order a copy, go to www.splendorinworship.com

Christ paid the price to set us free.

Title: Lenten Banner
Medium: Textile art
Artist: Natalie Lombard

A pastor wrote me:

"The theme we have chosen for this Lenten season is 'Behold Your King.' Christ whom we worship as our King is a serving and suffering king. He is tempted as we are, but is victorious. He pays a price for us, because we are sinners. He will not be turned aside from His march toward His coronation, exhibiting great love and compassion for His people as He proceeds toward His hour. Our Lenten worship culminates in His coronation.

"While I have outlined some specifics of this Lenten series, we would like this banner to be appropriate for any Lenten series in future years. The Cross should not be prominent if used at all. The cross or other instruments of suffering are only dimly perceived at the beginning of Lent, coming into clearer focus only later. Rather, royalty should be suggested throughout, whether by purple, a crown, or whatever your imagination conjures."

Natalie reminds us that Jesus Christ said to feed His sheep. Trim away the grizzle and the fat in your design, cut and shape each piece of the food in the visual image for immediate comprehension, for beauty that draws the viewer to gaze and savor, for ingredients of theme, and details that challenge, captivate, and invigorate the viewer to a deeper life with Christ.

The Great I AM is the God of creation.

Title: Explosion of God's Love
Medium: Acrylic on canvas
Artist: Carmen Vera-Shababy

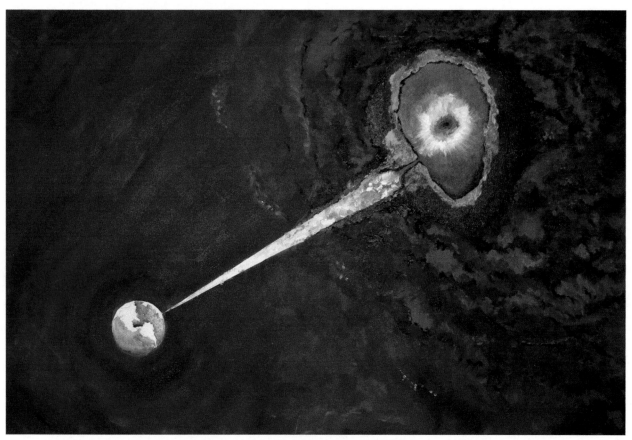

If we could see the spiritual manifestation of God's powerful love, what would it look like? This is what I envisioned when portraying God's never ending love.

His Word says, "For God so loved the world that he gave his one and only Son, that whoever believes in him shall not perish but have everlasting life."
— John 3:16

We know that Jesus was God's gift of love manifested in fleshly form. God is continually pouring out His love upon the earth, whether corporately or individually, His love never fails to exist!

Carmen's biography, advice and contact information are on page 33.

Yahweh is the beginning and the end.

Title: In the Beginning
Medium: Acrylic on crumbled paper
Artist: Carmen Vera-Shababy

This piece of prophetic art was truly God inspired and done spontaneously at an art workshop. The media is acrylic paint on wet crumbled paper. It represents the "Trinity" through the symbolic gemstones.

God the Father is represented in gold, which depicts His majestic position. Jesus is red, which symbolizes His precious blood. And the Holy Spirit in green, which means the peace of God. Here the Holy Spirit is shown hovering over the expanse of the earth going to and fro.

"In the Beginning was the Word, and the Word was with God, and the Word was God." — John 1:1

Christ knows the longings of our soul.

Title: The Movement of My Love
Medium: Acrylic on paper
Artist: Carmen Vera-Shababy

The poem that the Lord gave Carmen, as she captured the essence of this leaf, instead of painting it botanically correct, applies to all of us who struggle to be free in the art we create. And as you stare at her art, the leaf turns into a bird flying into the freedom found in Jesus Christ — who breaks the rope that ties us down.

> *"Even as you are attempting to be so detailed*
> *you will never be able to duplicate My creation.*
> *Only I can duplicate My own creation.*
> *Only I can see every detail, for you are like a leaf.*
> *I see your every detail, every color, variation.*
> *I see the depth of your heart, your cares, your flaws.*
> *Trust in Me as you are swept away!"*

Jesus blesses us when we acknowledge Him as Lord.

Title: Worship
Medium: Acrylic on canvas
Artist: Carmen Vera-Shababy

"Worship Me, worship Me, worship Me," were the words spoken by the Lord to me during a time of prayer. At that time, I was going through a difficult situation in my personal life.

Since then, the vision and these words have been an anchor for my soul. When your focus is on Jesus, and not on the circumstance, all else will seem to disappear. Surrendering the situation and willfully reverencing our Lord and Savior, will result in a much needed strength to endure and persevere through life.

"Exalt the LORD our God and worship at his footstool; he is holy."
— Psalm 99:5

"Shout for joy to the LORD, all the earth. Worship the LORD with gladness; come before him with joyful songs."
— Psalm 100:1-2

Biography

Roughly 25 years ago, I had a divine encounter with the Holy Spirit. It was then that He revealed that He wanted me to paint for Him.

Although I've been called many years ago, I continue to humble myself before the Lord so that I can be teachable and trainable. It is only then, that I can truly be used mightily for Him!

I love to teach children the gift of prophetic painting. I'm available for workshops and/or small groups. When not teaching painting, I'm an elementary substitute teacher. I reside with my daughter in a western suburb of Chicago.

Contact Information

Email: paint4iam@yahoo.com

Advice

It is always best to allow God to show you what's on His heart for you to paint. He will not only give you what to paint, but also the name of the painting and the meaning behind it.

A prophetic painting, drawing, artwork etc., is one where it is God created, directed or inspired solely by Him. Wait upon the Lord and He will indeed renew your strength.

Our loyalty belongs to Christ.

Title: KNIGHTSTAR
Medium: Pencil
Artist: Justice Carmon

Copyright © 2011 Justice Carmon. Used with permission.

"Put on the full armor of God, so that you can take your stand against the devil's schemes. For our struggle is not against flesh and blood, but against the rulers, against the authorities, against the powers of this dark world and against the spiritual forces of evil in the heavenly realms." — Ephesians 6:11-12

Years ago, my school had a mascot called "The Charger Knight," as we were the Chargers. He had a lightning bolt sword and helmet. I liked him and drew him for the school newspaper. I was smitten at the time with Star Wars, Iron Man and ROM Spaceknight — you can see all those elements in his design. When we briefly moved to Texas, I was forced to modify him into a pure Knight of the Stars [Blackstar and Firestar were popular Saturday morning cartoon characters at the time].

Later, I re-visioned the character as an astronaut who went on a secret space mission and ended up being involved in a galactic war, fulfilling ancient prophecies about a "Thousandth Knight" from a "world of wars" [Earth, naturally].

But over the last 30 years, as I have come to know Christ personally, I have seen my view of this childhood creation more as the "spiritual man" I want to be — a protector of the weak, wise in thought, fearless in action, the first to fight evil and the first to seek peace, well-armed with the sword of truth and willing to use it at need.

Christ commands THIS warrior indeed!

Biography

Justice Carmon holds a B.F.A. in Communication/Fine Arts from the University of Memphis. He was born and raised in the land of Elvis by Presbyterians, a Bible in one hand and comic books in the other.

Residing in Wheaton, IL, he now serves as a Bible teacher, caregiver, and storyteller for Jesus. He has written for Clubhouse Magazine, DevoKids, Jordan House [through Livingstone Books] and just finished his first 12-page black and white mini-comic "The Dragonknight" for *Possibilities*, a writer's group journal.

Justice was the Visual Arts Department Head for the 2012 Karitos Christian Art Conference.

Contact Information

Blog: justicecarmon.blogspot.com   Facebook: https://www.facebook.com/justice.carmon

Advice

Spend much time feeding on the Lord's goodness and mercy to you, to strengthen you as you struggle with the World. Meditate on His Word and keep in mind FIRMLY that God created you to be sensitive and wise, not overly-sensitive and whiny.

Whenever asked to do something, do it. It is far more important that you do bad art than waiting until you are able to make perfect art. "Abraham went out, not knowing wither he went." We are supposed to go into the unknown and discover. When someone says they love your art, say, "Thank you!" Then be quiet. If they want to know more, they will ask.

Beware of narcissism. The moment you cannot enjoy another's art that is vastly different from yours is a red alert. You can be creative AND responsible. You can be on time. You just have to pray more and set more alarm clocks to help you.

Whenever you feel your artwork is un-appreciated, talk to God. His usual answer: "Yes. Me too. Stinks, doesn't it?"

The Holy Spirit comforts us and lifts us up.

Title: Pathway of Promises
Medium: Acrylic on canvas
Artist: Brenda Tarasenko

This was a painting I did over Remembrance Day. The Lord was speaking to me about releasing the suffering of the lost. It personally was about grieving my father, who lost his arm in Dieppe, and suffered emotionally throughout his life.

Corporately, it was about all our sorrow being an acceptable offering to The Lord.

As we lay them down to Him, it paves a way to Heaven.

Remembrance Day is a memorial day observed in Commonwealth countries since the end of World War I, to remember the members of their armed forces who died in the line of duty.

Biography

After asking the question, "What is my purpose and gifting from God?" I found myself on a journey of hearing His Voice through art. The more I stepped into saying "YES" to the doors that opened for me, the more I developed a burning hunger to share His message with others.

Brenda is an artist and facilitator who lives in Ontario, Canada. Here is a great quote from her website: "She [Brenda] knows that art is a wonderful tool that can effectively unlock the gifts of those who are actively growing in the prophetic."

Contact Information

Website: brendatarasenko.com   Email: beauty7ul@me.com

Advice

The best advice I've heard yet, to getting started, is to lay down my concerns about how the art should look. This sets me free to enjoy the process!

Christ prepares His bride.

Title: Preparing the Bride for His Coming
Medium: Acrylic on canvas
Artist: Brenda Tarasenko

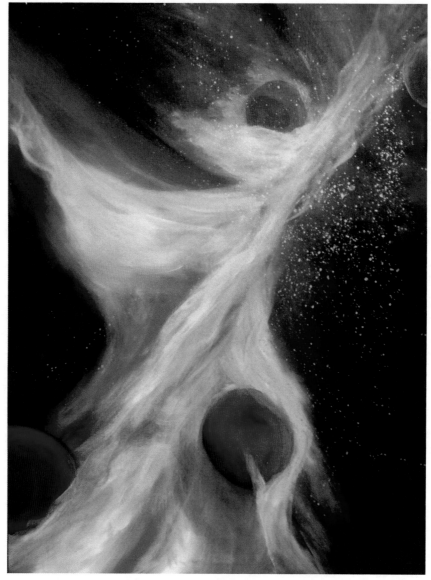

This is another one of my recent works. It has the four blood moons, which is a current sign of the times.

Special Note: Red moons will fall on the Jewish Passovers: April 15, 2014, and April 4, 2015, and on the Feasts of Tabernacles: Oct. 8, 2014, and Sept. 28, 2015.

Christ's blood sets us free!

Title: Untitled
Medium: Gold and natural ruby
Artist: Steve Nelson

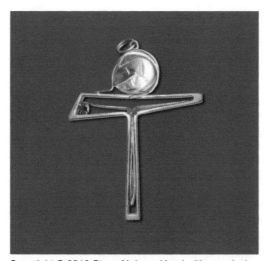

Several years ago, a priest asked me to make a crucifix — a cross that shows Jesus hanging on it. Because Jesus is alive to me, I like to show Him alive in all I do, and was given permission to design a stylized cross. The ruby on the left side symbolizes Christ's blood. The lines in the head have a double meaning — they are the closed eyes and show the bridge of Christ's nose, and also form the shape of a smaller cross.

The priest made a request to his family that when he passed away, the piece of jewelry should be returned to me. His family honored the request.

Biography

I went to a public grade school in Chicago, and private high school. There wasn't much of an art program in the public school, but I won a scholarship to the Art Institute. For the next two years, I spent every Saturday morning at the Art Institute. In high school, I was into athletics, but continued to do art.

At Wheaton College I majored in the sciences, but found a way to marry art and science. It happened one summer in the Black Hills. I met a person who wore the most amazing jewelry. When I asked him where it came from, he said he made it. For the rest of the summer, he mentored me in the art of jewelry making.

When I returned to college, I took a metal sculpture class so I had access to a torch. I graduated with a major in biology and a minor in chemistry. With a lifelong interest in art and science I thought metal smithing might be a temporary way to make a living.

Today, I'm a goldsmith, silversmith, diamond cutter and GIA-Graduate Gemologist. I spend most of my time designing custom jewelry. My business is *Sierra Gem Network, LTD*, and my studio and showroom are in West Chicago, Illinois. Because I'm a diamond cutter, most of my work is making engagement rings. I call it "matrimonial hardware."

When I'm working on a piece of jewelry for a customer, my mind goes to the person who will wear it. I pray for that person while I work. I've always been a 3-dimensional artist. I only draw out of necessity, but I sculpt in my sleep!

Contact Information Email: diamondsforyou@gmail.com

Advice

Keep producing your art, no matter what. A good source of inspiration is to watch other artists and see what they're doing. Use this as inspiration only; don't be a copycat. Try to discern early on what your particular style is. Remember that you are not the first person to draw a circle.

The Holy Spirit helps us persevere.

Title: Untitled
Medium: Ink and gouache on paper
Artist: Phillip W. Hoagland, II

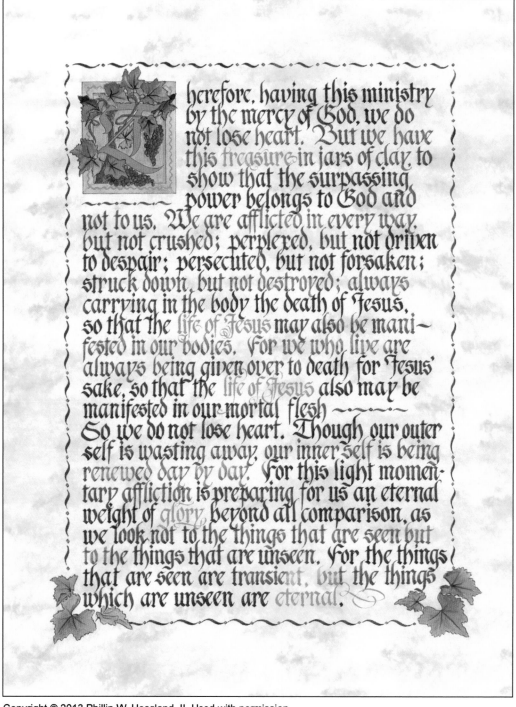

This piece was done as a gift for my Pastor. His wife, sons, and one of his nephews were badly injured when their van was rear-ended; that same week his father was hospitalized for emergency quintuple by-pass surgery.

Some weeks afterward, he shared with us at a men's retreat how he had been hanging onto this Scripture for encouragement and strength during the dark days that followed those events. These words from Paul's second letter to the Corinthians became a defining Scripture for his life. I knew at that moment I wanted to present him with a rendering of those words to serve as a reminder of God's faithfulness during that time and for all eternity.

For this piece I chose Fraktur lettering, which first appeared in German manuscripts about 1400. The letter forms contain many sharp points, like the thorns of a briar, which seemed to be an appropriate representation of the many painful trials that the apostle was describing. And yet when they are put together, these pointy letters create a beautiful, ordered page, full of substance — which is only fully appreciated when you pull back to take the whole page into your view. So it is with our lives.

A few words relating to our promised eternal reward have been written with gold metallic ink to highlight and associate them, and to provide a visual contrast to the earthier flesh and blood colors used for the bulk of the text.

I also used purple to both indicate the royalty of the name of Jesus, and tie in the color of the grapes — the fruit which is also crushed — but which in time, produces the finest wine.

Biography
Phillip Hoagland teaches Theatre Arts and Humanities at Doss High School in Louisville, Kentucky, where he lives with his wife, Maura, and their four children. Calligraphy has been a favorite part-time hobby for about thirty years.

Contact Information
Email: philandmaura@gmail.com

Advice
I believe that our creative tendencies are a reflection of God's creative nature; but it is essential that we are not primarily creators, but His creation. When we meet our obligation to love Him first and foremost, then our creativity is more likely to be used in ways that honor Him. In the words of Augustine: "Love God and do as you please. For the soul trained in love to God will do nothing to offend the One who is beloved."

Close up of Phillip Hoagland's illumination.

The Lord stirs our hearts to bless others.

Title: Homeless Jesus
Medium: Acrylic on canvas
Artist: Dale Olsen

This painting was completed in a one hour worship service. The objective was to give a visual voice to the teaching and Scripture of the day.

The teaching was from Matthew 25, "the least of these" and how we see others around us. I chose a combination of abstracted forms to indicate the background of a building and a hurried, moving crowd, and the more realistically rendered light pole, curb and figure to create the visual context of a vibrant busy cityscape.

In the sequence of painting the work, I intentionally waited to the very end of the painting to fill in what everyone thought would be a generic homeless person. Their comments later told me that the green army jacket was expected but things changed when the robes and sandals took shape. The face of Christ (painted last) shown downcast, sitting at the curb anonymously, is to show how easily we look past others, not seeing them as children of God, loved by their Creator and just as valued by God.

This work created more conversation than any other worship painting that I have done. I think that the Spirit was using it when one person said to me, "I won't see a homeless person in the same way after looking at this painting."

Biography
I was that kid who could draw and paint. God used a time of illness in my life to give me the time to begin developing as an artist. I am an architect and muralist, in addition to being a fine arts painter.

Contact Information
Website: daleolsen.fineartstudioonline.com

Advice
I would call visual artists to four tasks. They are not listed in any order of importance, but they are all critical.

First, become as proficient as you can in your artwork. Study art history, take lessons in your preferred medium, work as hard as you can to be as excellent as you can be. Get advice and critique from outside your family and your church (while there you may be the art person and likely more talented than others, you need to get another measurement of your skills and your eye).

Secondly, study the Word. Become familiar with the Scriptures — their flow through Biblical history, and the connections of the themes, stories and concepts. Intensive Bible study will prepare you to give a visual voice to Biblical truth.

Thirdly, listen for the Spirit's promptings and act on them. Carry a small sketchbook with you as you are in a Bible study or a worship service. Draw in church. Is there a visual image to what is being preached? Draw it out. Then develop it later. The sketchbook/journal may hold images, notes and concepts that you will come back to later. Follow the Spirit's leading.

Lastly, be open to taking risks. If asked to paint during a worship service, take the risk and do it. I did, and I found God used my work to inspire others. When you take risks, you will grow.

Jesus Christ is Lord over all.

Title: LORD
Medium: Acrylic on canvas
Artist: Dale Olsen

This smaller, 24" x 48" derivative work is based on a mural sized, 6' x 16.' The original mural hangs in our church's main fellowship hall.

The "wordscape" came from the inspiration received during a Bible study of the life of Moses. Each week's lesson would end in a question that asked what attribute of God do you see in this week's lesson. After a time these attributes rang out like a drumbeat. I began making a list of the words. God was prompting me before I knew a painting would result.

Some construction was taking place in a very visible spot in our church where a barrier wall was needed. During a break, while attending a meeting in our church, I was asked if I could come up with some temporary decoration for the wall. The meeting was droning on, and I began drawing instead of listening. The artwork that resulted was done on a large canvas that could be relocated once the project was finished.

This image of words interlaced and layered shows attributes of God surrounding the main title word, Lord. The background colors are the colors God chose for the first place of worship: the maroon, blue and purple of the Tabernacle. The words are all in metallic finishes, and reflect light as the viewer moves past the artwork. Behind all the words is a thin gold leaf cross.

It hangs in a heavily used multi function space. I have received feedback from many people, most often telling me how they see a word in the painting that speaks to something they need in their life at that time.

Jesus died for our sins.

Title: The Substitute
Medium: Mixed media: acrylic, magazine photos, textured paint
Artist: Mitzi Blanchard

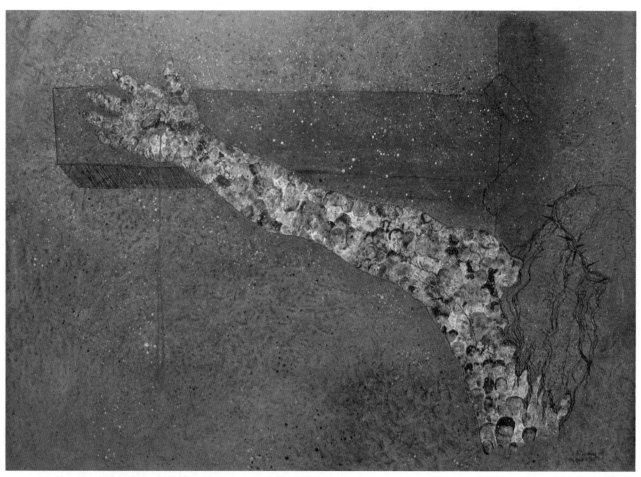

The Holy Spirit downloaded this image into my heart many years ago during a worship service. The body of Christ, on the cross, is made up of many faces which I tore out of magazines.

The message is: He died in our place; it should have been us.

Mitzi's biography, advice and contact information are on page 49.

God's wisdom is better than earthly desires.

Title: Bigger Barns
Medium: Mixed media
Artist: Mitzi Blanchard

This piece came about as a result of a challenge given in our church art fellowship. We were asked to choose a parable and illustrate the truth of it as the Lord illuminated it to us.

Mine is based on Luke 12:13–21, the Parable of the Rich Fool. As you can see from the wagon full of stuff, he has amassed a great fortune. Rather than being generous with the abundance God has given him, he has it all tied up and is transporting it to a larger storage place. His glasses are lying on the ground, as he has lost his focus. The path ends at a drop-off, and the balloon (representing his soul), is about to be popped. The picture illustrates the foolishness of being selfish toward others and toward God, because in the end it's all left behind for others anyway.

Then someone called from the crowd, "Teacher, please tell my brother to divide our father's estate with me."

Jesus replied, "Friend, who made me a judge over you to decide such things as that?" Then he said, "Beware! Guard against every kind of greed. Life is not measured by how much you own."

Then he told them a story: "A rich man had a fertile farm that produced fine crops. He said to himself, 'What should I do? I don't have room for all my crops.' Then he said, 'I know! I'll tear down my barns and build bigger ones. Then I'll have room enough to store all my wheat and other goods. And I'll sit back and say to myself, "My friend, you have enough stored away for years to come. Now take it easy! Eat, drink, and be merry!"'

"But God said to him, 'You fool! You will die this very night. Then who will get everything you worked for?'

"Yes, a person is a fool to store up earthly wealth but not have a rich relationship with God."

— Luke 12:13-21 (NLT)

Christ shows us the way.

Title: The Way Beyond The Cross
Medium: Mixed media
Artist: Mitzi Blanchard

This piece came to be as the result of a challenge given in our church art fellowship: to create a "stained glass window" that would relay a truth we wanted people to know. "The Way Beyond The Cross" is seen as if standing just under the cross (the brown border at the left and top).

It illustrates the path we walk as Christians, sometimes through the desert, sometimes not seeing the forest for the trees, but always with the Holy Spirit alongside, until we come to our true home, represented here by the gold castle walls.

Biography
I have been "arting" since I was old enough to hold a crayon. I am primarily self-taught. I love to experiment with many different facets of creating art, including collage, papermaking, and assemblage. My productivity has ebbed and flowed with the demands of life, but I am coming into a new season of freedom and inspiration and creativity.

One of my heart's greatest joys is creating opportunities for emerging artists to discover their creative gifting.

Mitzi has served on the steering committee and as a volunteer for the Karitos Christian Arts Conference for many years.

Contact Information
Email: mitzi.blanchard@gmail.com

Advice
My advice to any Christian artist is this: Allow the Holy Spirit to breathe life and truth into your work, whatever form it takes. I have experienced more fulfillment in creating a simple piece that speaks volumes of truth than in twenty pieces that are "pretty."

Holy is the Lord.

Title: Angel
Medium: Watercolor art
Artist: Zahava Raz

Copyright 2011 Zahava Raz. Used with permission.

After being inspired by an angel picture, this idea came to mind. It is an attempt at a different way of painting an angel. Many of my angel drawings are simple in form, but this one is a more finished piece of portraiture. The cropping makes it more powerful because it gives a close-up of the essence of an angel.

I painted it while babysitting my grandchildren. They had gone to bed and I had time to kill. People have to realize this kind of art isn't necessarily created under some kind of mystical experience. Much of it is natural ability given by God combined with a desire to paint something that would give glory to Him.

I think prophetic art has to do with "intention" — what comes out of the heart that is already there. Some prophetic artists are seers and visionaries. I don't always see things that clearly. I pray, get an idea and then search for pictures to help me form a drawing. I'm greatly inspired by other prophetic art. I know when I see it. It tugs at my spirit.

Biography

I am a portrait artist and a prophetic artist. I've drawn and painted all my life, especially faces. I can copy things well and have a developed "eye." I had art lessons as a young girl, and have had some college courses in advertising and design, but for the most part, I've been self-taught. I have also worked in other media: batik, wood block prints, oils, silkscreen, and some acrylic. Most of all, I like pencil and watercolor. I work mainly in portraits from photos. Recently I have begun to explore prophetic art. I pray before my art begins, asking the Holy Spirit to inspire me with ideas and knowledge of how to do it. Then I just use the talents He gave me to create something beautiful.

Zahava taught two portrait art workshops at the 2011 Karitos Christian Arts Conference. Her workshops were well received, and one lady was delivered from the fear of drawing during one of her classes.

Contact Information
Email: zahavaraz@comcast.net

Advice

I am still learning about prophetic art. One thing is for sure: the artist must have the "intention" of creating something for the Glory of God and making the art as "praise" unto Him.

Christ is supreme!

Title: Revelation Jesus
Medium: Colored pencils
Artist: Zahava Raz

This is a sketch of Jesus as described in the Book of Revelation. It was a spontaneous, spur-of-the-moment drawing that came to mind after finishing an assignment in a prophetic art workshop of creating art on a dark background. I had time left over, and the idea came to mind to sketch the Revelation description of Jesus with a white pencil. So I made Christ's hair "white as wool" and gave Him flames for eyes. I did not draw the sword coming out of the mouth. It was a very quick drawing, almost unfinished. I was unpressured when I drew it, and it just came out of me!

Later, this piece of art was displayed in the narthex of Faith Lutheran Church in Geneva, Illinois. Many people were drawn to look at it.

God watches over His creation.

Title: Ezekiel's wheel
Medium: Acrylic on brown paper
Artist: Zahava Raz

"Ezekiel's vision." The idea formed in my head as I closed my eyes and saw two interlocking wheels with eyes as described in Ezekiel. Interlocking wedding rings.

The Holy Spirit speaks life into our hearts.

Title: The Heart of God with Flowers Coming Forth
Medium: Fabric and trim on cardboard
Artist: Zahava Raz

This is the first piece of art I did in one of Lynn's art workshops. This idea formed as I worked on it and I kept adding flowers to depict them coming out of Jesus' Heart.

After I finished the art, I went to a worship service at Praise Ministries Inter-national and saw a view of my picture as it was really meant to be. I had a vision of Jesus with His Arms outstretched. His Heart was filled with flowers floating towards me, symbolizing the gift He is sending me from His Heart. This picture speaks to me a lot.

The Glory of the Lord covers the earth.

Title: Radiant Glory
Medium: Acrylic on paper
Artist: Zahava Raz

I want to know about God's glory — to see it, feel it and be in it. I was trying to capture the essence of Glory depicted as light that radiates living Light.

The Lord fills our empty nest.

Title: Robin's Nest
Medium: Digital art
Artist: Lynn Zuk-Lloyd

One day, I discovered a robin's nest in my backyard. It was so thrilling to see a nest with blue eggs snuggled in the bushes, I had to draw it. Although this piece of art didn't start out with any awareness on my part of the Lord prompting me to create it, the Holy Spirit used it.

Two years later, while I was gathering stuff together to speak at a women's luncheon, the Lord told me to give away three of my art prints prophetically. Then HE brought to my mind, the three HE wanted to use, with the robin's nest being one of them.

At first, I panicked! I had never done anything like this before. What if people thought I was crazy? What if I looked foolish? What if no one wanted the art prints? Fear gripped at my throat. I felt the Lord urging me to do what HE asked. Finally, I agreed, knowing that the only way to overcome fear is to do what I'm afraid of doing.

So the next day, after making my presentation, I cautiously said, "There's someone in this room who feels like their nest is empty. The Lord wants you to know that HE is going to fill your empty nest and replace what was taken away — what the locust have eaten." Then I held up the art print and added, "If you feel the Lord is speaking this message into your heart, this picture of the bird's nest is for you."

A lady lifted her hand with tears in her eyes. "That's me," she cried, gratefully accepting the art print.

Lynn's "Robin's Nest" art also appears in her book, *The Garden of God's Promises.* Using exquisite, full-color prophetic art and tender, God inspired stories, author/artist Lynn Zuk-Lloyd offers stepping stones of encouragement for Christians facing worry, fear and stress, or who simply need a place to rest. Her book contains 40 illustrations, 40 stories and over 100 Scripture promises to bless, strengthen and uplift. Lynn's book is available on Amazon.com.

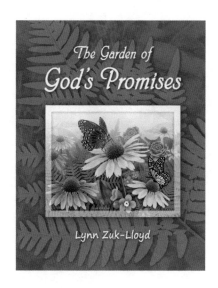

When we lose our way, the Lord comes after us.

Title: Rescued by the Lord
Medium: Digital art/photography
Artist: Lynn Zuk-Lloyd

In our search to find meaning in life, we can wander into the wilderness of differing opinions, get stuck in the swamp of negative thinking, and loose our way. But when we cry out to the Lord, HE comes and saves us. HE rescues us again and again, just like the many examples of God's faithfulness in Psalm 107.

"Rescued by the Lord" was shown at the December 2013 "Reflections" juried art show at Arterie Fine Arts Gallery in Naperville, Illinois.

This piece of art also appears in Lynn's book, *The Garden of God's Promises*, and is one of her most popular art prints.

Biography

Lynn Zuk-Lloyd is a prophetic artist, author and speaker who loves to help people snuggle closer to Jesus. She understands the benefits of practicing listening prayer, honing art skills, and growing in the prophetic.

In 2006, two publishers at a Christian writer's conference told Lynn to combine her art, design and writing skills to develop her own line of books. After taking the idea to the Lord in prayer, she plunged into the publishing arena, and now has three non-fiction books, a novel, a children's Christmas book, several short stories, and three art books.

In 2010, the Lord prompted Lynn to take her paintings and speak to groups willing to listen to what HE gives her. She now speaks at women's breakfasts, luncheons, job clubs, ministries, and Christian business groups.

The Lord also opened doors for Lynn to teach prophetic art at conferences: Deborah Champions, Karitos Christian Art Conference, Karitos INDY, and Releasing Prophetic Arts. She's had the privilege of being the Visual Arts Department Head for Karitos 2011, and served on the Karitos steering committee for several years. Lynn's art has been exhibited in the Philadelphia area and at shows and galleries in the Chicago suburbs.

She holds a BFA in Advertising Design. In 2012, she received her minister's license from Praise Ministries Church. Lynn served on the prayer and ministry healing team at Faith Lutheran Church, and worships with other artists at Living Stone Christian Church.

In 2014, she appeared as a guest on Don Albert's "Everlasting Love" program on Chicago cable TV, where she talked about the Lord speaking to people's hearts through art.

Lynn loves to encourage artists. She organizes gatherings and monthly art workshops where artists share concerns, listen for God's Voice, create art, and have fun.

Motivational speaking has become one of Lynn's favorite things to do. She welcomes opportunities to speak, teach and lead art workshops. Her books are on Amazon.com.

Contact Information

Website: www.promisegarden.com   Email: lynn@promisegarden.com
Blog: http://encouragementlady.blogspot.com

Advice

It takes time to grow faith, develop talent, and hone skills. Practice art and spend time with the Lord as much as possible. The closer you walk with Jesus Christ, the better your ability to hear and see what the Holy Spirit is doing. Because God is beautiful, the art we create needs to be beautiful. Take classes whenever possible. Connect with other prophetic artists for community, prayer and support. They need you and you need them.

God sets us free from things that constrain us.

Title: Ice Encrusted Leaf
Medium: Digital Photography
Artist: Lynn Zuk-Lloyd

Copyright © 2011 Lynn Zuk-Lloyd.

Curled up like a cocoon, the ice-covered leaf hangs from a branch in quiet solitude. The icicle at the bottom of the leaf stretches outward, like a hungry tongue.

Why is this leaf so hungry-looking? Is there unseen beauty waiting to emerge from its protective covering? Or is the leaf looking for more to life?

There is always more to life than what we see. There is also great beauty that lies within each of us that is hungering to come out.

Too often, we only see the dryness of our lives. We may think the best years have past us, and try to wrap our hopes around the things that are close at hand.

But the best is yet to come. For these are the days the Lord is speaking life to dry bones. HE is calling HIS people to rise up and come forth. Jesus Christ is bringing out the beauty HE placed deep within us, and releasing the Kingdom of God through us. And all who want to be part of this adventure are welcome.

This photograph, and the words of encouragement, are on display at Faith Lutheran Church in Geneva, Illinois.

The Holy Spirit encourages us to look up and "see!"

Title: Christmas in North Woods
Medium: Digitally created illustrations
Artist: Lynn Zuk-Lloyd

Prophetic art takes on a new characteristic when the Lord places the idea on our heart to illustrate HIS love in graphics that will bless children. And when HE gives us the idea, HE makes the way possible.

When my children were little, I wanted to write and illustrate a Christmas book containing fun stories that also kept Christ in Christmas. It didn't happen. More than twenty years later, when my grandson turned five, the Lord nudged me to refine the characters I had experimented with, edit the stories I had written, and publish a Christmas book. With the help of the Holy Spirit, *Christmas in North Woods* became a reality.

Christmas in North Woods contains twelve fun, delightful stories that not only entertain, but also honor Jesus as Lord and Savior. It's available on Amazon.com.

The Holy Spirit awakens our spirit.

Title: Lion
Medium: Acrylic on paper
Artist: Barbara Velez

"You are precious and honored in my sight." — Excerpt from Isaiah 43:4

For the background colors, I chose pink and a blue. Pink because I'm a friend of God, and blue for revelation. As I pondered on the Scripture verses, I saw hands holding a heart. As I painted the heart, I felt lead to paint some type of light or rays symbolizing His light into my heart. But then suddenly I felt the need to add red and orange symbolizing praise and the fire that comes from being in His presence. Then I added the three jewels symbolizing the Trinity and unity — God in three persons touching my heart and changing it.

Suddenly, as I stared at the piece, it became clear that if you look closely, the art looks like a lion. I just felt that the Lord was telling me, "I'm the Lion of the tribe of Juda, and I am with you," and He reassured me that I'm His beloved.

Biography

The Reverend Barbara Velez is a teacher and intercessor. She has worked in the ministry of helps since 2001. Her ministry is focused on teaching others how to honor and serve Apostles in and through diverse areas of administration and intercession. Barbara is a passionate worshiper with a prophetic anointing. She seeks to honor God and minister praise and worship through the arts.

Contact Information

Email: roblesdejusticia@hotmail.com

Encouragement

Several years ago, someone asked me about the prophetic arts and this was my response. Art is an expression of God's heart and word in a visual way. It is also an expression of our hearts towards GOD. In other words is a form of communication and worship expression.

Can art be prophetic? You can see in the Old Testament that God used many different ways to express His word to the prophets. He even had the prophets act in odd ways to deliver His message.

Today the Lord keeps speaking to us and through us. In Hebrew, the word traditionally translated as prophet is NEVI, which likely means "PROCLAIMER." We are all to be proclaimers of His word. As we hear His voice we must choose to proclaim it. Therefore, the Prophetic Arts allow us to release what we are hearing from God, by proclaiming it in a tangible way.

People that move in the prophetic can use words, music, art and other media to visually illustrate what they are hearing from God. I find it interesting that 1 Corinthians 13:9 talks about our knowledge being partial and incomplete, and even the gift of prophecy reveals only part of the whole picture!

Don't hold back! GOD has given you the ability to create, and there is always a way to create an expression that will serve as worship and as a proclaiming tool. Art allows us to do exactly that.

God assures us of His Victory!

Title: The Cross
Medium: Acrylic on paper
Artist: Barbara Velez

This piece of art was supposed to be a thank you note from the traces of paint left by the lion's paint. As I looked at it, I felt led to add brightness using yellow and orange to the background. And as I started to draw the "T" for thank you, it reminded me of the cross. I immediately thought about the Victory we have in Christ Jesus by the Cross. So I added the purple "V" for victory. There is a lot to be thankful for. Psalm 70:4 (NKJV) "Let all those who seek You rejoice and be glad in You; And let those who love Your salvation say continually, 'Let God be magnified!'"

Jesus shatters the walls that imprison us.

Title: Thy Mysterious Movement
Medium: Acrylic on canvas board
Artist: Shirley Mize

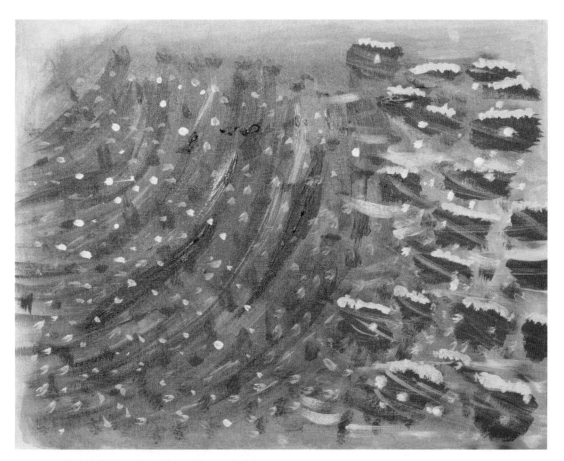

There is mystery in this painting. The Lord meets us in the storms. The movement on the left side of the painting represents the Holy Spirit. On the right side, there are individual bricks with mortar on top of each brick. As the Holy Spirit moves, the bricks pull apart and the walls that keep us trapped, tumble down.

The Lord causes joy to burst forth.

Title: Garden of Joy
Medium: Colored tissue paper
Artist: Shirley Mize

"He makes my feet like the feet of a deer; he causes me to stand on the heights. He trains my hands for battle; my arms can bend a bow of bronze. You make your saving help my shield, and your right hand sustains me; your help has made me great." — Psalm 18:33-35

This piece of art represents joy, jubilation, celebration and life. I created this art in one of Lynn Zuk-Lloyd's prophetic art workshops, where we painted with glue and tissue pager.

Biography
I have always loved art. In grade school, I created a piece of abstract art and my teacher loved it. Most of my life, I never had the opportunity to have professional training. But now, in later years, I'm stepping into art and discovering there is great joy when you create art. It's like you are partnering with God. Most of my paintings involve leaves, trees and landscapes.

Advice
Keep doing art, even though you feel like you don't have the training or the skills. There is a deep mystery to art. Step into that mystery with God.

Jesus heals our wounds.

Title: Leaves of Healing
Medium: Acrylic on canvas using real leaves
Artist: Shirley Mize

A friend encouraged me to do art with leaves because leaves represent healing. I grew up in a wooded neighborhood with prolific, blooming dogwood trees. So this type of art was enjoyable because it reminded me of the woods. The movement in the background represents the Holy Spirit, who stirs up leaves of healing to bring life into our lives.

The Lord transforms us into His likeness.

Title: Expectancy
Medium: Acrylic on paper
Artist: Shirley Mize

Transformation means things aren't the way they used to be. We may long for transformation, but only God can bring it about. I've been longing for transformation. And when I started this painting, the word, "transformation" would not fit, so I wrapped it up the side and around to the top of the paper. This was good, because transformation is never the way we expect it to be. It is much better. It is the way God calls it to be. I am thanking God ahead of time, in advance, before things happen, expecting areas of transformation to take place.

We are beautiful in God's eyes.

Title: SUSIES SALON
Medium: Needlepoint
Artist: Gwendolyn S. Fullenwider

A favorite memory of mine is seeing my mother doing all the little girls hair in our kitchen the day before Easter. This was my inspiration for creating SUSIES SALON. They would come into our home with washed, coarse hair filled with naps. Momma would press each girls hair with a pressing comb and then she would curl their hair with her curling iron. The pressing comb and the curling iron were both heated on her stove.

Each girl would leave smiling, looking so pretty with her freshly styled hair. Momma filled them with so much joy.

I created SUSIES SALON from a drawing I drew, and graphed it to be stitched.

Biography

As a child, I taught myself how to do needlepoint from books that I initially got from the library. Later, I purchased books.

This love of needlepoint, and wanting to create affordable and original pictures for my home, lead me to creating my own pictures from my drawings and photographs. I have used my needlepoint, artwork and photographs to create greeting cards using the gifts that God has blessed me with. My goal is to start my own greeting card company.

Gwendolyn is a talented artist who participated in the prophetic art classes at the Karitos Christian Art Conference.

Contact Information

Email: gwenful2@sbcglobal.net

Advice

My advice to artists is to use the gifts God has blessed you with. Learn as much as you can about your craft. Do what you can do now, until you are financially able to do more. Love and enjoy what you are doing.

God sets our feet dancing!

Title: Count It All Joy
Medium: Mixed media on canvas
Artist: Amelia Whaley

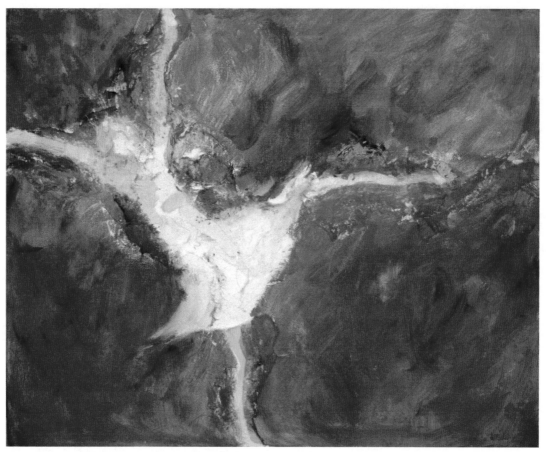

This painting was created at a conference at St. Andrews Church, Mt. Pleasant, South Carolina. I had sketched an abstract cruciform design earlier and began this piece by glueing different papers in the cruciform design for texture. As I painted with different shades of my favorite color red, suddenly I saw a female figure begin to take shape. She exuded freedom and joy. As she was taking shape, I heard the keynote speaker say, "We were born to worship God, and we can worship Him with our entire body!"

For the first time, I realized that I was painting in real time — painting what the speaker was saying as he was saying it. The only way that can happen is through the unity of the Holy Spirit.

Biography

Amelia Whaley began her painting career in 1985 with a Christmas gift of watercolor lessons from her father. Amelia lives in Mt. Pleasant, South Carolina. She leads the Real Time/Worship Painting Team at St. Andrews Mt. Pleasant. In addition to painting at worship services, she also paints during conferences and special events. Her original artworks are part of several church collections in the United States. Additionally, Amelia enjoys leading day or weekend workshops in watercolor, watercolor journaling, collage and the release of creative play.

Contact Information

Website: www.ameliawhaley.com

Advice

(a) continually grow in deeper relationship with the Lord through Scripture and prayer, (b) grow in your artistic skill and (c) be alert and open to the opportunities the Lord will bring your way.

Christ assures us that we are important.

Title: Vessel
Medium: Mixed media on wood panel
Artist: Amelia Whaley

This painting was created as part of my series, "Altered Settings: Unexpected Beauty in Timeworn Fragments" for a larger art show called, "Infusion," sponsored by Artist on Fire and the Piccolo Spoleto Festival in 2011.

I was inspired by aged and damaged pages from manuscript illuminations from the middle ages, that I had seen on a trip to Paris. The pages were quite beautiful, even in their damaged state, speaking to me of reality and humanity rather than "perfection."

When something is broken, damaged or shows imperfection, we, as a society, normally choose one of three options to deal with "damaged goods." First, we can salvage or preserve it, depending on the perception of worth or importance.

Second, we can discard, devalue or even destroy it. The third way is to introduce, integrate or infuse it into another form, creating something new that could not exist without the attributes of the damaged item.

I created illuminated pages in a manner authentic to the time, using vellum, natural pigments with egg as binder, 23 karat gold leaf and dip pen and ink. After aging and distressing a page, I incorporated it into a larger work of mixed media on wood panel, changing the nature of both the illumined page and the wood panel. The integration high-lights the beauty of the illumined page, even in its damaged condition, much as a setting for a precious stone.

Each of us is a vessel, an imperfect one — broken in places and bearing scars — but always valuable because God created each of us in his image. And He is gifting us in unique ways for His purposes.

This piece is owned by a woman whose young daughter had been born with a birth defect; she wept when she recounted how she knew of other children who were unwanted because of defects. "Vessel" was an affirmation that true worth, beauty and purpose have little to do with appearance and "perfection."

Close up of Amelia Whaley's painting.

God is a God who blesses.

Title: The Wrestle for a Blessing
Medium: Oil on Canvas
Artist: Suja Jacob

This painting is about the day Jacob was upgraded to "Israel," at his wrestle with the angel of the Lord. To my surprise, even after I painted this, I saw the verse in Hosea 12:4, that he earned the Lord's favor with his tears.

Yes! He will never despise a prayer out of a broken and contrite spirit.

"So Jacob was left alone, and a man wrestled with him till daybreak. When the man saw that he could not overpower him, he touched the socket of Jacob's hip so that his hip was wrenched as he wrestled with the man. Then the man said, 'Let me go, for it is daybreak.'

"But Jacob replied, 'I will not let you go unless you bless me.'

"The man asked him, 'What is your name?'

"'Jacob,' he answered.

"Then the man said, 'Your name will no longer be Jacob, but Israel, because you have struggled with God and with humans and have overcome.'

"Jacob said, 'Please tell me your name.'

"But he replied, 'Why do you ask my name?' Then he blessed him there."
— Genesis 32:24-29

Biography

Suja Jacob was born and brought up in Kerala, India, and moved to the U.S. in the late 90's. She graduated in Fine Arts from the prestigious Stella Maris College, Chennai. She has held several Art Exhibitions/ Fairs in India and in the U.S.

Suja is a member of Naperville Art League and is active among the artist community in the Naperville/Aurora, Illinois area. She is a regular participant in art fairs conducted in Promenade, Bolingbrook and the Mayslake Peabody Estate. Suja gives art lessons, for kids and adults.

She says, "I am thankful to have the gift to paint. I loved to paint since childhood. My dad, who passed away three years ago, celebrated me as an artist."

Contact Information

Website: www.sujajacob.com   Email: sujasijil@hotmail.com

Advice

Try to do something positive!

Christ's great love for us goes beyond our understanding.

Title: Potter & the Clay
Medium: Oil on canvas
Artist: Suja Jacob

This is a painting of Mary Magdalene, as she squanders her alabaster jar of perfume upon the feet of her Master. Did she even know, that soon, He was to squander every drop of His blood upon that cross for her?

"While Jesus was in Bethany in the home of Simon the Leper, a woman came to him with an alabaster jar of very expensive perfume, which she poured on his head as he was reclining at the table."
— Matthew 26:6-7

Jesus gives us eyes that see.

Title: Mary Magdalene at the tomb of Jesus
Medium: Oil on canvas
Artist: Suja Jacob

Mary Magdalene, "a sinner" as the Bible comprises, with the narration of the disciples mental thoughts as she anoints the Lord's feet, is enough to set our imaginations wild.

Yet, she, being blessed to see the resurrected Savior, even before the disciples, speaks plainly about the story of any saint — "saved sinner."

If any of us think, "I am a sinner, I am not worthy of Christ, He's holy and pure," that is when we become most eligible for Jesus Christ.

God refines us like silver and makes us beautiful.

Title: Untitled
Medium: Acrylic on brown paper
Artist: Risa Bauldauf

And the words of the Lord are flawless, like silver purified in a crucible, like gold refined seven times. — Psalm 12:6

And a man with a shriveled hand was there [in the synagogue]...Then he [Jesus] said to the man, "'Stretch out your hand.'" So he stretched it out and it was completely restored, just as sound as the other. — Matthew 12:10 &13

I will refine them like silver and test them like gold. They will call on my name and I will answer them; I will say, "They are my people," and they will say, "The Lord is our God." — Zechariah 13:9 b

I will give you treasures hidden in the darkness — secret riches. I will do this so you may know that I am the Lord, the God of Israel, the one who calls you by name. — Isaiah 45:3 (NLT)

This tree was painted on a crumpled piece of brown paper. Just as God unshriveled the hand of the man in the synagogue, He unshrivels us as we trust in Him. — Matthew 12:10-13

I opened the crumpled paper that was given to me, painted the tree and the light behind it, and used aluminum foil to make the leaves. Through adversity and hardship, God is purifying my faith and refining me as silver (Psalm 12:6). The jewels at the bottom are the treasures that He gives us that are hidden in the darkness. My life has been much darkness, but God is bringing in His Presence to lighten my darkness (Psalm 18).

I am grateful and watching how God will bring more of His presence to me and to my family.

The Lord pulls us out of deep waters.

Title: Rising out of dark waters
Medium: Paper and watercolor
Artist: Risa Baldauf

Copyright © 2013 Risa Baldauf. Used with permission.

God lifts us higher than the waves of darkness that threaten to pull us under. He rescues victims of domestic violence and tends to the brokenhearted. He lifts those who trust Him above the trauma of incest, away from sexual abuse, and beyond the feeling of guilt over not being able to protect their children. He lifts the downtrodden higher and higher than the onslaught of anger, confusion, self-pity and feelings of worthlessness.

Yeshua, the Risen Son of God removes our shame. He places friends in our lives to help us keep looking at Him. He strengthens our shield of faith, and helps us to know that He loves us and will always love us, even when destructive forces try to do otherwise.

Trusting Him to bring us to complete wholeness and healing is a continuing process. But He is faithful, patient, thorough, wise and powerful. He works on our behalf. And the good work that He started in us, He will bring to completion.

Christ sets the prisoners free!

Title: Breaking the Chains
Medium: Acrylic on canvas
Artist: Christine Cole

This painting depicts the freedom from sin and bondage that Christ gives us when we receive Him as our Lord and Savior. It was done for a show by ex-cult members, and it depicts my journey of being in a cult and then getting set free from it (I was actually kidnapped by my two best friends and deprogrammed).

It is very powerful visual for people who have experienced bondage in their lives, and many people have been very moved by it.

Biography

I have been fascinated with nature and color and have been drawing and painting since I was a small child. After receiving my degree in biochemistry, I returned to my first love and studied fine art at the Ontario College of Art, as well as studying with several professional artists in Toronto. I love to paint in plain air and create inspirational pieces.

More recently, I've been painting live on stage during worship services and conferences at various churches. I love to paint with the Holy Spirit — what the Lord is showing me.

I live in Ontario, Canada.

Contact Information

Email: jcpcole@yahoo.com

Advice

I would advise other artists to paint what you know, and be true to who you are. Paint what moves you.

The Lord delivers us from evil.

Title: Stairs of Time
Medium: Acrylic on Canvas
Artist: Christine Cole

This painting was started live on stage during worship at a conference at my church, and then finished several months later in my studio.

Prior to heading out to church to paint, I received a vision. I saw stairs coming down from top to bottom. They were colored in rainbow hues. A small black snake (representing Satan) was at the second stair and a figure was climbing up to the second last stair. Blood poured down from the red stair. Pink clouds rained down blood, water, fire and oil. There was lightning flashing above and an emerald rainbow. I sensed that the stairs represented time. We were almost at the end of time; we had one more stair to go. Then the stairs suddenly rolled up in a white scroll and time was over. The vision ended.

I presented this painting at an arts/worship meeting and many people were encouraged and impacted by the Lord in a positive way.

More Advice

I would advise artists to keep painting what the Lord shows you. I suggest that you find a mentor or pastor/leader who can encourage your gifting.

I was very displeased with the first draft of this painting and quite discouraged about my calling and talents as an artist. Soon after, I was asked by someone in leadership about the message of the artwork. She told me that the message was important for the body of Christ, and I was encouraged to finish the piece.

Jesus crowns us with compassion.

Title: Crown of Thorns Pendant
Medium: Wax sculpting and metal casting
Artist: Brad Ferguson

On Christmas Day, 1997, I gave my girl-friend, Debbie, a pendant I'd fashioned for her. She was stunned by its beauty and suggested that maybe I was supposed to make jewelry for a living. She sketched a design and asked if I could make a pendant that looked like her drawing.

The next day I set my simple wax sculpting tools on my study hall desk and sculpted the Crown of Thorns pendant. I knew there was something more than my hand at work in the sculpting process. An idea came to mind that the number of thorns on the pendant should be thirty-nine, symbolizing the traditional number of lashes Jesus received when He was scourged. I started counting to see how many thorns I needed to add or remove. There were exactly thirty-nine thorns!

I could hardly wait to take it to Debbie for her approval. She was impressed. It was exactly what she had pictured in her mind. She was even more amazed when I told her my story about the number of thorns. We were both convinced that God had guided my hands in the sculpting process.

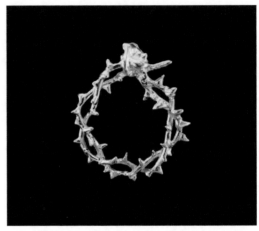

Copyright © 2013 Brad Ferguson. Used with permission.

After the Crown of Thorns pendant was cast and polished, we noticed another un-planned symbolism. The pendant was also a circle that intersected with itself seven times. The circle represents eternity. Seven is the Biblical number for perfection and completion. Thus, our Crown of Thorns pendant symbolizes God's eternal gift to us, the perfect and complete atonement for our sins that Jesus made through His suffering and the shedding of His blood. Wow! We didn't plan any of this. HE did!

Biography
I grew up in Texas, where I also went to college and earned a Bachelor of Science degree in psychology and sociology. I grew up in church, but wasn't truly born again until 1976. I started my jewelry business, *Samaritan Arts Jewelry* in Amarillo, Texas in 1980, and opened my website in 2000. I displayed my work at the Christian Book-seller's Convention twice, and had a sales relationship with American Family Radio for five years.

Contact Information
Website: www.SamaritanArts.com   Email: Brad@SamaritanArts.com

Christ seals us in His love.

Title: Signet Purity Ring
Medium: Wax sculpting and metal casting
Artist: Brad Ferguson

In 1998, Debbie and I were asked by someone at church to make a purity ring with a subtle design. Purity rings were becoming increasingly popular, and so we began talking about designing a line of them. We prayed and asked God to help us. He gave us a concept for a different type of purity ring — a signet ring.

First, we designed a line of rings where the tops were cut into various emblems. Each emblem was a special symbol reminding the wearer of the commitment to remain pure until marriage.

Then, as I was driving home one day, an idea sprang into my mind. If these were going to be signet rings, we needed to provide not only sealing wax, but also a commitment card which the young person could sign and then seal it with the ring until the wedding day.

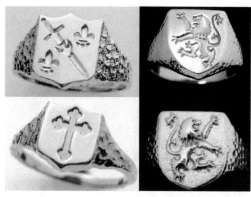

When I got home I told Debbie the idea. We both felt that God had given me this idea of the sealed commitment card to complete the concept of the Signet Purity Ring design.

Advice

1) Artists create. Create what you are passionate about.
2) Be disciplined, and work hard at your craft so others can see what you see.
3) If you intend to make a living with your art you MUST acquire business skills, or hire someone to run your business. YOU are the business. Your business is how your art gets seen and promoted. And the money you make gives you more freedom and opportunity to do your art. Read books about business from a Biblical perspective. And make sure you acquire a working knowledge of the paperwork side of business.
4) Make sure you have someone who believes in you — someone who will encourage you in your creating and in your business.
5) Acquire people skills. See others as your friends and not your opponents or competitors, or worse, a bother or distraction. The wider your circle of friends, the more successful you will be.
6) Exercise and expand your creative nature to learn and to improve! One way to push yourself to create is to commit to selling or exhibiting your art in a public forum.
7) Attempt projects that you don't know how to do. You will learn from the process. Creating is not a passive thing. It is active. It uses energy. It uses you.

The Lord nestles us in His protective Arms.

Title: Bird's Nest
Medium: Felt, fabric and twine
Artist: Susan Zimmer

Warmed by the glowing Son of God, the tree's winter grayness turns into delicate buds and green leaves. A bird's nest, tucked into the hug of two branches, holds tiny eggs waiting to burst open with chirps of life. Fluttering feathers fall from parent birds, who hurry to and fro with feedings. These feathers symbolize God's

unending, protective care for His creation.

I developed an affection for trees, birds, and bird nests. To me, they represent life, and symbolize how to rise above difficult situations when there is pain and darkness on the inside.

When I was a child, my bedroom was on the second floor of our house. Outside my bedroom window was a great elm tree. This "tree of mine" lived in the narrow strip of grass between the concrete sidewalk and the asphalt of the street. My elm had an arm-circling trunk — tall, thick, and strong. The majestic trunk was topped with a maze of mighty branches and leaves.

From my window, I looked into those mighty branches, reaching out and up ... toward the heavens. I enjoyed seeing the fresh green leaves that unfolded in the spring — like butterflies emerging from their cocoons, the deep green foliage in summer — green, just like my eyes, the fading greens and yellows and tans of autumn — like a bright section of the color wheel. I didn't like the cold, gray barrenness that winter brought to my tree.

In spring and summer, the warm sun filtered through the leaves, sending into my bedroom multi-colored reflections of dancing shadows. These images were moving dapples of sun and breezes, showing me that outside was alive.

My father was abusive. My tree was a safe place of escape, to sit on an upreaching branch, to rest against the solid strength of the trunk, to be hidden among a covering of leaves ... in my imagination. My elm saw; it knew; it sheltered me! I did not know Jesus as my Savior then. I did not know He was my shelter, my protection.

Years passed ... I grew up, I married, and I moved into the home my husband had built — a wonderful place hidden in the midst of an acre of great trees!! Standing

at our kitchen sink while washing dishes, looking out the window, I became aware of birds, nests, little families up in the tree branches ... alive.

One warming spring day I saw a robin fly past the kitchen window, with a long stem of dried grass stuck on her beak. I wanted to help her ... little did I know! I watched, my eyes moving upward with her flight to near the top of a box elder tree. I hoped she wouldn't get stuck among the branches and little spring leaves. Wow! She didn't have a stem stuck to her beak, she was carrying it ... to a nest she was building!

Over the next several weeks, I watched this Mother Robin. She finished her nest, settled in snugly for a few weeks, and then was joined by a busy Mr. Robin. They had a little litter of hungry baby birds to feed. These parents flew out and in, almost non-stop, taking turns feeding, tending, nurturing, protecting their growing babies. (Psalm 91:4)

Now, I know Jesus as my Creator, my Savior, my Lord. I turn to Him (Psalm 91:15) for my needs (Psalm 23:1), my security (Psalm 91:5), my peace (Psalm 91:1-2). I praise God for the beauty of His creation! (Genesis 2:3)

A dream of mine is to have a tree house of my very own, high up in the branches of one of our mighty trees . . . next to a bird nest would be delightful, a snug little place to nestle in with a favorite book, on a sun-dappled day, whiling away an afternoon ... someday ...

Biography
Susan is a multi-talented, retired teacher who is creative both indoors and outdoors. She is also an excellent editor.

Advice
Use experience in your life to create beauty.

God helps us discover His treasures.

Title: Shagbark Tree
Medium: Pencil
Artist: Janet Hart Heinicke

I believe that this tiny planet we inhabit together, with other human beings, is a marvelous revelation of the mind of God. Careful observation of the growing plants and of the living creatures on earth reveal (to me) a beautiful order, a "design" that is harmonious and pleasing.

So, whenever I discover some new growing plant, tree, animal or bird, I rejoice and seek to discover and understand just how that new discovery (to me) is put together. Doing so is always a joy, a kind of celebration that the hymn writer penned in, "How Great Thou Art."

This drawing of a shagbark tree in a nearby forest preserve provided just such an opportunity! My intention is to share that discovery with my viewers.

Biography

I am a life long artist and teacher! For twenty years I served as chairman of the art department at Simpson College, located in Indianola, Iowa. Prior to that time, I was coordinator of the art program at Kankakee Community College, and previous to that experience, taught at Judson College and Elgin Community College.

Since I love to teach (AND LEARN BY TEACHING), I continue to teach as a faculty member in the museum school attached to the Des Moines Art Center.

I find exhibiting my work provides me an incentive to continue working in the studio, and so have in my exhibition record more than 100 one-person shows, and a record of acceptance and exhibition in competitive venues.

My travels, exhibitions and teaching experiences have extended out of the country to eastern Europe, Africa and the Far East.

Janet holds a Master of Fine Arts in Painting, a Master of Science in Art Education, specializing in printmaking, and a Doctor of Education. She has attended numerous seminars and classes, including workshops on Japanese paper making, watercolor painting, and monoprint etching and soft ground. She has received numerous honors and awards for her art, and has been listed in Who's Who in America (2007 to present), Who's Who in American Art (1986 to present), Who's Who in the Midwest (1981-1992), and International Woman of the Year (2001 to present).

Contact Information
Email. janetheinicke@earthlink.net
Website. www.janethartheinicke.com

Advice
Always keep making art. It is a universal language and provides you a tool that speaks without words!

The Lord's ways are wonderful!

Title: Pool at Usangi
Medium: Pencil
Artist: Janet Hart Heinicke

In the last two years, I traveled back to East Africa to once again visit friends and co-workers in the Pare Diocese of the Evangelical Lutheran Church in Tanzania. Since this was my seventh such journey, I said to myself, "This will be my last trip; I will help those traveling with me to establish their friendships while I am here, but this will be my last journey."

We visited the Usangi Training school, where evangelists are trained for work in parishes, and while there, were taken to see a big structure which was to become the church for the parish. It was big enough to seat several hundred people, there were no windows and no floor yet. But, African like, I was told with absolute confidence, that it WOULD be completed, though funds for the church had not yet been raised. And at present, there are less than fifty students at the school. To me the church embodied the kind of complete faith and confidence that God would provide — so characteristic of the African Christians I had met.

In this church, I saw a big wall, and of course, said what any artist would say,

"that wall needs a painting!"

By six p.m. the same day, I had been taken to meet the pastor. Plans were in the works for me to come back and do such a painting. The pastor said that he wanted something in the painting to suggest the Holy Spirit, baptism, and communion.

I came home thinking, "Wait a minute, this is God's work! I never planned to return to Africa, nor to paint a large painting for a church there. But ... there it was! What do you want me to do GOD?"

I returned to the Midwest and to Iowa. My husband's health deteriorated; I began a series of negotiations long distance to provide a painting.

This pencil sketch is the first proposal submitted for that task. Since light often seems to me to suggest the Spirit's presence, the area of light represents the presence of God, and the pool of water, like one I saw near Usangi, the found presence of baptismal water. I hope the final images submitted in late 2013, will do what I can only regard as "God's work."

Jesus Christ is our Source of Living Water.

Title: Life River
Medium: Mixed Media
Artist: Brian Russelburg

This work is a little different than what I have done in the past. It's a little more like an illustration and simple, but I believe simplicity can sometimes be strong.

This is my finalized copy for the show "Reflected Light: A Midsummer Art Exhibition 2013." It's composed of Enamel paints, Acrylic paints, a tad bit of water color paint and montage photographs, that I assembled in Adobe Photoshop. All drawings, paintings and photos were shot and painted by me.

From an airplane you can always tell where water is located. From the window of the plane you may see flat checkered fields, but you also see the meandering evidence of watered streams. All along the edges and on both sides of these streams grows lush foliage. It's as if nothing grows too far away from this life giving water, but on the edges of these streams life is abundant.

Nothing thrives if placed too far from the water. The stream IS life. It's probably no accident that the nature, direction and angles these streams take, resembles that of our own vascular system in our bodies — bending here, cutting across there, and jutting around turns.

Like these streams, our veins were also designed to feed our bodies with the necessary nourishment.

In Ezekiel 47, vs 1-12, the Bible talks about the Living Water which flows from the Temple and from every angle. All along these streams grows lush vegetation that is always in season and bearing unending fruit. Fish also thrive in this water.

The message to us is to stay very close to this Living Water which flows from the temple. It will nourish us and keep us in peace and health. Jesus is that Living Water, and we are encouraged to dwell next to Him, partaking of His water and thrive. But if we live apart from Him, we dry up.

Biography

Brian Russelburg received his Bachelors degree from Herron School of Art and Design in Indianapolis, Indiana, majoring in Fine Art Photography. He mixes the mediums of paint with photography to create impressionistic imagery. He has been a Christian since 1982 and has been married for over 28 years to Marlene Russelburg. He resides in Plainfield, Indiana, and attends Bread of Life Church in Avon.

Contact Information

Email: silvervisage@gmail.com

Advice

Being from the Herron Art School of Art and Design, we had many influences from professors and professional artists. But I heard good advice about following your heart and creating your own ideas, no matter how different they were. This I believe is what has already been planted deep inside you. Father God is the Creator, and He put those ideas in you. Everything that we see on this earth which is breathtakingly beautiful was created by Him. He will give you things to artistically create, if you are listening.

God's refining fire burns off lies and deception.

Title: Contagious
Medium: Colored tissue paper
Artist: Evan Okpisz

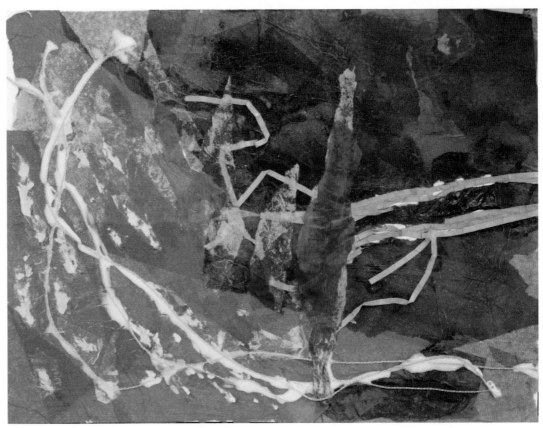

Copyright 2013 Evan Okpisz. Used with permission.

We are the torch in the center of the picture. Our flame is big on our own, but cannot conquer much. If you surrender to God, He will "blow" like the blue streams of air and spread the fire into a roaring flame. It will consume everything else.

Biography
I am a teenager who simply likes art, and I want to learn how to be a better artist. Ever since my first prophetic art workshop though, I learned the difference between a prophetic artist and an artist who does the art for himself or herself.

Advice
Let God flow through you and give you the art. Don't rely on yourself. Never look down at your own art because God always has a message!

Christ, the Lion of Judah, is King!

Title: Lion of Judah
Medium: Oil on canvas
Artist: Paula MinGucci

Copyright © 2011 Paula MinGucci. Used with permission.

The Lord directed this painting as I saw a picture in my mind as to what it would look like. Then He told me what to do with the background, and gave me the colors to use. I also saw a flaming angel in the studio during the painting process.

Biography
Mom of three daughters, loves to soak, worship and do prophetic art as well as graphic design and illustration. I'm currently taking prophetic commissions. I will prophecy to you using a painting or drawing.

Contact Information
Email: SevenSonStudios@yahoo.com

Advice
First, I would recommend getting an art education or learn to draw well. Then go through inner healing and soak often in the Lord. Begin to ask Him for pictures. He will give you that "seeing" gift where He gives you visions and inspiration. Also recommended, is becoming interested in prophecy and going to classes on learning how to prophesy.

Jesus calls us into His throneroom of grace.

Title: Hebrews 4:16 Banner
Medium: Fabric, trim and felt
Artist: Dale Baker

My banner was created in response to two separate requests that came within a week of one another. One person wanted a banner for the prayer room at the art conference. The other person wanted a banner to hang permanently in the prayer room at my local church. It was a blessing that I could use the same banner to fit both needs! It was very natural for me to create this special piece because I am a prayer warrior at heart.

Dale put a lot of prayer and tender loving care into the creation of this large banner.

The Lord used it to bless and deeply touched those who took time to reflect on the words and art, as it hung in the prayer room at the 2013 Karitos Christian Arts Conference. When people walked up to the banner, they could feel an anointing from the Lord.

At one point, people started singing prophetically next to the banner. Others walking through the hallway heard the music and joined in, blending their voices in a beautiful harmony of worship to Yahweh. The presence of the Lord filled the room. It was a holy moment.

Biography

I did not grow up attending church. Neither did I have any relatives, neighbors or friends who believed in God. But when I was radically saved at the age of 21, I was introduced to the Bible.

My banner making evolved from a deep love for the Word of God. My artwork springs from a life dedicated to prayer, Bible study and Christian fellowship.

My inspiration comes from many sources: 1. The Word of God, which is full of amazing imagery. 2. All of nature and creation. 3. Time spent in art galleries and antique shops.

I am 100% dependent on the Holy Spirit to lead me to the right materials for my banners and to help me assemble everything attractively.

It has been a great delight for me to create banners that bear Scripture. Many times I have seen God use His Word displayed on my artwork to touch lives!

Advice

Dedicate yourself to a life of prayer, Bible study and Christian fellowship. Be inspired by the Word of God and what Christ places around you. Depend on the Holy Spirit to lead you every step of the way.

Close up of Dale Baker's banner.

The Lord brings us into His Light.

Title: Teen Challenge Banner
Medium: Fabric, trim and felt
Artist: Dale Baker

Through the ministry of Teen Challenge, Jesus Christ saves young lives from alcohol and drug addiction. One day, as I was reading Psalm 107, I realized how well verses 13 and 14 illustrated the powerful ministry of Teen Challenge. With God's help, I created a banner that depicted the verses and mailed it to Chicago Teen Challenge. The banner was hung in one of the ministry rooms as a daily reminder to the students of God's ultimate goal for their lives — being totally set free from all chains of the past and walking in the Kingdom of Light.

"Then they cried to the LORD in their trouble, and he saved them from their distress. He brought them out of darkness, the utter darkness, and broke away their chains." — Psalm 107:13-14

Close up of Dale Baker's banner.

The Holy Spirit enables us to grow.

Title: Grow
Medium: Watercolor on crushed packing paper
Artist: Audrey Pryst

God, I think, works in funny ways. I created this project outdoors on the ground on a sunny day, not really sure of what to paint. And so, I followed the old kindergarten plan: if in doubt, make a flower, a butterfly or a rainbow. There wasn't any great booming inspiration from the heavens, just sunshine and a happy day.

Then, while I debated the addition of a butterfly or a sun to my singular flower, a fluffy dog ran across the painting, joyously licked me and left behind a lovely brown paw print. This mark, in lack of any other inspiration, I hid in the center of a second flower.

After fussing over my two flowers for some time, I was debating what else to add to my rather sparse artwork when I clearly heard God say, "Grow." I knew this was my title and that the picture was finished.

For me, I marvel at the way my spirit knew the plan and guided my hands even without telling my soul. There is such a strong sense of the small, wild-headed flower gazing up at the calm, orderly elder flower giving critical instruction. And when I asked, "Which flower is the one being commanded to grow?" I sensed that they both are, and that they each need each other to grow to the greatest heights. One grows through receiving, and the other through the giving — each role in its proper season.

Biography

I don't really perceive myself as an artist wanting to serve the Lord. Rather, I am a worshipper who happens to use art as a way to encounter God and to commune in intimacy with Him. I enjoy this, because every project then bears fruit, always and primarily in my own heart, but often and secondarily in the hearts of others.

Audrey Pryst currently worships God through art, dance, writing, knitting, and running (crawling, climbing, leaping) Spartan Races (you know, the ones with the mud, barbed wire and flames). She is just finishing the rough draft of her first novel, "Justice Rising," but refuses to give a publication date because God hasn't given her one yet.

Contact Information

Email: audreypryst@yahoo.com

Advice

God is really fun. He also wants us to be real and I've discovered that my most powerful projects are the ones in which I have exposed the exact things I would never ever want anyone to know. The willingness to go past the happy-happy-joy-joy art into the places where fear, hurt and pain generate not only a deep intimacy with the One waiting to meet us there, but also creates a rich anointing with the capacity to bring true healing to others. And *that* is really great.

The Lord's understanding is beyond our grasp!

Title: Island
Medium: Watercolor on wet crushed packing paper, plus other elements
Artist: Audrey Pryst

My original goal, the day I made "Island," was to try wetting my packing paper before painting on it, as an attempt to control color placement. Packing paper is fairly slick and gravity had caused me some troubles in the past. Instead, I discovered that wet, waddy paper gave an entirely different surface that somehow communicated in a new way, creating the sense of earth and land. I don't really know what "Island" means, just that everyone who looks at it gazes for a while, likes it, and recognizes that it has an anointing. This reminds me of the Scripture, "But the natural man does not receive the things of the Spirit of God, for they are foolishness to him; nor can he know them, because they are spiritually discerned." (1 Corinthians 2:14, NKJV). Maybe one day God will unfold the meaning to my soul, but for now, it is just a mystery with a weight on it.

The fire of God's heart protects us.

Title: The Fire Wall
Medium: Oil on canvas
Artist: Gelene Keever

This is the very first painting I did with God. I put on worship music, got out a canvas and oil paints, and said, "Ok God, let's do this." I was so proud of how it turned out. I had never painted with oils before this. It was like He took my hand and guided it across the canvas stroke by stroke, each one masterfully placed to create the finished product which I call "The Fire Wall."

Biography
Gelene attends a large church in Pennsylvania where many artists sketch in their seats. Afterwards, they gather together and share what they drew.

Contact Information
Email: sognare13@yahoo.com

Advice
Do what you love to do! Don't be afraid to take risks and try something new. Mix mediums: acrylic and watercolor, ink and crayon, marker and puffy paint...there are endless possibilities. Try new techniques and have fun with it! Create from your heart and let the vision inside you come alive!

The Holy Spirit deepens our roots in Christ.

Title: Untitled
Medium: Markers
Artist: Trisha L. Stern

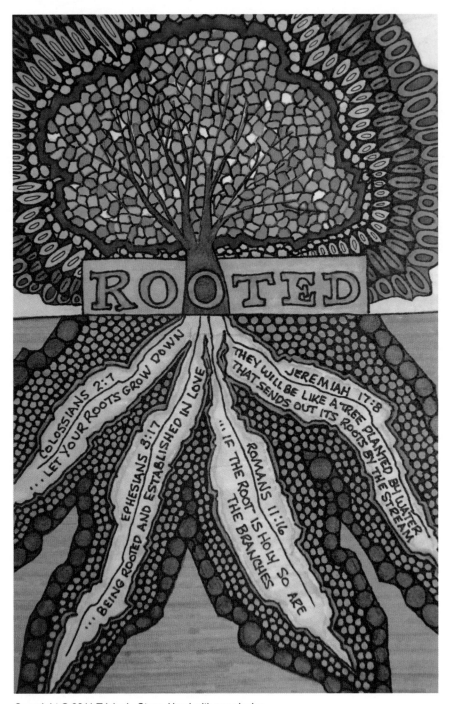

This piece of art was a response to the Lord impressing the importance of being grounded and rooted; it is the depth and development of our rootedness in Christ that sustains our faith. This illustration is a visual of how important good, solid roots really are. We often look at the crown of a tree and stand in wonder, yet totally miss that it is the root system (out of sight and beneath the surface) that is key to the tree's growth and survival.

This really spoke to me; I thought at first it was a personal word only, so I was totally unprepared for how others responded. People were able to instantly relate to this picture, and several have commented that they have a better understanding of how important spiritual roots are. I love that people "get it" when they look at it; it's like they have an "aha moment" and the concept just clicks. That is so exciting!

Biography
Trisha Stern is an artist, teacher/speaker, writer and avid gardener. Her prophetic art was birthed in personal trauma several years ago; it was a gift God gave her in a time of great emotional pain, and was instrumental in her healing process.

Contact Information
Email: trishals1@yahoo.com

Advice
Your intimacy with the Lord is absolutely key! Worship. Pray. Listen for His voice and for His leading — and then move forward. His is ever faithful.

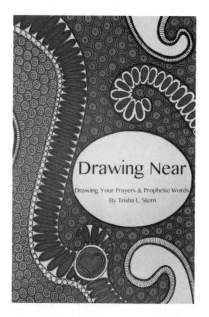

Trisha is working on her first book entitled, *Drawing Near: Drawing Your Prayers & Prophetic Words.*

Jesus pours out blessings upon us.

Title: Untitled
Medium: Markers
Artist: Trisha L. Stern

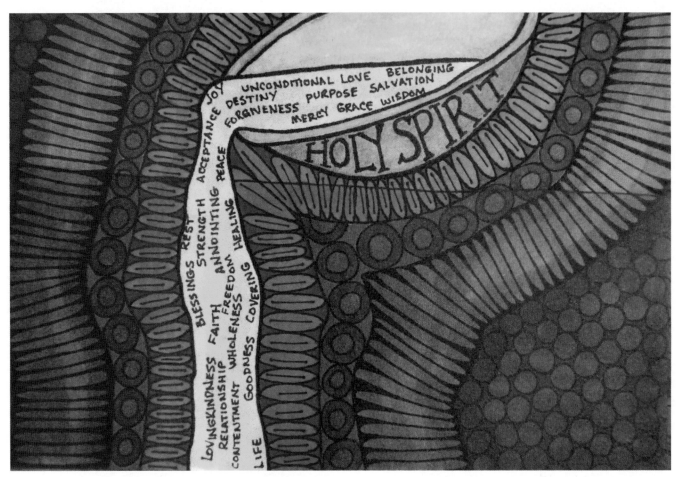

Copyright © 2011 Trisha L. Stern. Used with permission.

This drawing came out of an intense time of worship with the Lord. His presence was particularly weighty and comforting — like a thick, soft blanket. I saw a large, golden bowl pouring out blessings, but there was a wide barrier of some sort that prevented the people below from receiving those blessings. As worship continued, that barrier became narrower and narrower, until it was just a thin line that could not hold back the blessings that spilled through. Afterwards when I shared the drawing, someone said, "That's exactly what I saw!"

The Lord places praise in our hearts!

Title: Untitled
Medium: Markers
Artist: Trisha L. Stern

This is one of my favorites! In an extended time of worship, it felt as though I were in the Throne Room singing, "Holy, Holy, Holy." I experienced an overwhelming sense of awe and awareness of Who He is, and of how worthy Jesus Christ really is. I saw bowls filled with the worship of the saints being poured out before His throne and then refilled to be poured out again and again. I heard words and phrases of worship, and His names and attributes being thundered out. It was incredible and life changing, and when I look at this picture I experience it all over again.

The Lord watches over us and protects us.

Title: Tomorrow
Medium: Oil on canvas
Artist: Merike Adams

This painting is about giving and finding love and support in difficult times. There is a storm in the background of the painting. Everything is shifting, falling, sliding downward. The mother bird is holding the eggs in place. It is her love that protects when times are difficult. When we think we are all alone and lost, there is still hope in tomorrow when love supports us in the hard times.

Biography

My art is a journey. At times it is descriptive, at times statement-making, and at times it is deeply personal. My art is mostly about nature and people, expressing both the beauty and the sacred in nature.

I was born in Tartu, Estonia, received a diploma from the University of Tartu in Finno-Ugric languages, studied ceramics at The Ceramic Arts Studio of Christoph Hansing and Brigitte Jauss in Hamburg, Germany, started drawing and painting courses at the College of DuPage in Illinois and still continue my studies in art.

I have won several prizes for my art, such as "Best of the Show," "Best Theme," and several honorable mentions. My art is also part of private collections in Estonia, Germany, USA, and Canada. My mosaic sculptures and painted sculptures have been to several public art displays in Chicago area.

In 2004, I founded a small art business, "Color and Light."

In 2013, The Arterie Fine Art Gallery in Naperville, Illinois came to life. My dear friend JoAnne Larson and I operate Arterie, and offer monthly juried shows, solo exhibits and professional critiques to artists. In addition to the shows, Arterie offers quality art lessons for children and adults, art themed birthday parties, and gallery space for events.

Contact Information

Website: www.arteriefinearts.com

Advice

Experiment with your art. Don't be afraid to make mistakes. Sometimes we try to make things so perfect, we get stuck. But it's through mistakes and experimenting that we learn and become better artists.

God the Father lavishes His love on us.

Title: The Prodigal Son
Medium: Mixed media with watercolor pencils
Artist: Peggy Wilmeth Carr

Peggy Wilmeth Carr

Have you ever felt that God doesn't care about your losses? In Luke 15, God the Father is preoccupied with His losses, and He relates to everyday, important losses for the people of that day — a lost dowry coin, a lost sheep, and finally, a lost son. God leads us from our own silly values for inanimate objects, to a living being, and finally, to a person, with an eternal soul!

One Sunday morning, our instructor said, "Many people think this parable is about the Son, but really, it is about the Father. "That was confusing to me. My definition of "prodigal" didn't fit a Holy God, who would never backslide from His own teaching and commandments! The whole class leaned in, to hear more.

"You see,"the instructor said, "prodigal" means "lavish!"'

Slowly, I was comprehending this: God, the Father, is more lavishly abundant in His Grace, than we can be flagrant in abusing it! Our instructor explained how the father in the Biblical story ran to his son, with clothes and a ring, to save his son's reputation in the community. Not only that, he gave him a private reinstatement.

This art print was a pencil sketch that I hand-colored. It is God inspired art that people have gravitated to, and is part of the "Amish series." Let's receive God's lavish Grace!

Biography

Peggy Wilmeth Carr has been a Christian for over 50 years. She grew up in the Bible Belt, moved to Wyoming, and met new and wonderful friends there.

After the move to Illinois, in the 80's, God introduced her to a family of extraordinary and inspirational Christians, who intentionally raised their art in praise to God! While in Illinois, she served on the steering committee for the Karitos Christian Arts Conference. Peggy is now back in Oklahoma, to be near her parents. She is an artist, song writer, poet and worshiper of Jesus Christ. She loves children.

Contact Information

Email: write4almightypc@yahoo.com

Advice

God supplies everything. So start, and finish, what God has given you to do. Work on your placement for all the foundational parts of your composition before you begin to render.

If you think the art you created isn't good enough and you have done your best, figure out what needs to be corrected and correct it. But don't keep fussing over your art. Eat and go to sleep, so you don't ruin what you've created. Remember that NO ONE gets it right the first time!

God is the Deity, not the work of your hands. Be willing to let go of your art. And don't think that you will never be able to re-create something you have lost. What you create next may be better because You have the same Source for Anointing each day!

Prophetically, be sure you are called to do what you are doing, and not just trying to drum something up (2 Peter 1:10). Pray for the revelation that the Lord wants, and obey what He gives you. If the vision tarries, wait for it. (Habbakuk 2:2-3)

We may not have the Urim and the Thummim today, but we have the same God, who answered Gideon's fleece, and He is patient with us, until we "get it." (Judges 6:12-24, 36-40 and 7:12-15).

Last, please obey God's promptings quickly. We may never know what wonderful things we could have done. If you learn from my mistakes, I will rejoice!

Jesus places smiles on our faces.

Title: Untitled
Medium: Acrylic on paper
Artist: Tricia Rush

I never worked with paint before, and when I started the picture, I had an idea of how it was supposed to look. What I actually made was nothing at all like what I wanted. To me, it looked very juvenile and thin. Then Lynn rotated the painting each direction. It was interesting to see how something I planned out — that came out less than what I envisioned — turned into a different and better creation just by changing the perspective. It turned into a happy painting with smiles and fishes representing what Jesus calls us to be: happy in Him and fishers of men.

Biography

I enjoy designing and incorporating workshops geared toward creativity exploration, music/rhythm, interpersonal communication and self-expression. I also enjoy Scottish Gaelic, photography, balloon twisting, playing Mrs. Santa Claus, and playing the Hammered Dulcimer.

I am certified in Education, Library Science, Team-building/facilitation, Youth Management Techniques, and Music Education.

Contact Information

Email: miahdulc@yahoo.com

Advice

My advice to others would be that if it's not working out the way you thought it should, just look at it from another angle — a new direction. Let go of preconceived ideas. It's interesting to see what the possibilities then become!

The Lord calls us to action.

Title: Red Horse
Medium: Acrylic
Artist: G. Antonia

This was a moving vision. I saw a rolling green pasture with a small dot far off on the horizon. Larger and larger it became, until I could see that it was a most beautiful red horse. It continued to gallop toward me and turned to the North just before we collided. I called out to the Lord "Oh Lord what a beautiful Horse!"

Immediately the power of God fell in my room with such power it was almost frightening. Waring in the spirit began with my prayer language taking over. I was never given the exact situation but I knew a battle had been won. The Lord had wanted immediate prayer.

Biography

My name is Gail Antonia Simons, and I paint under the name of G. Antonia. I am a licensed Minister and attend Praise Ministries International Church in St Charles, Illinois. I became a Christian at age 11 and have had a wonderful and amazing walk with the Lord. I am happy to share my attempts at portraying the beautiful visions I have been given through these paintings.

Contact Information

Email: ladylion7@hotmail.com or through my church

Advice

I find that when I move immediately upon inspiration, I do my best work. I would suggest all aspiring artists do the same. You can always adjust the painting later, but get the initial image down as quickly as you can.

I must admit that is not always possible. If it is God inspired the image will be planted on your mind with no release until the painting is done. So don't worry!

Jesus calls us to feed His sheep.

Title: Feed My Sheep
Medium: Acrylic
Artist: G. Antonia

This painting is the focal point of a much grander vision that was similar to watching a full color movie. The Lord was in a large green pasture with a multitude of sheep. The wind was blowing, a few sheep stepped forward to be fed. The Lord stooped down to feed each one individually out of his hand. Human beings would just fill a bin with food or throw stacks of hay and then leave. The attention the Lord paid to each individual sheep is what I wanted to portray with this painting. Over the vision like a headline were the words, "Feed My Sheep." The amazing part of this interactive vision was as each sheep came forward to eat out of the Lord's hand, I felt their lips on my own hand!

Now a few years later, I understand the vision. I now mentor incarcerated young men (one at a time) at the Kane County facility in Illinois. The Lord works with me and the boys eat God's word right out of my hand. Our work is done through the Kairos Torch prison Ministry. The Lord is still asking us to Feed His Sheep.

Yahweh writes the symphony of creation.

Title: Only The Master's Hand
Medium: Colored pencils
Artist: Matt Lawlor

Only the Master's Hand can direct and complete the harmony of heaven and earth...

Copyright © 2013 Matt Lawlor. Used with permission.

Early in the year of 2013, I began to receive prophetic pictures that began with the earth. The earth with its massive number of people and its many countries readily testified to its complexity. The many languages and ethnic diversities, and the geographical variety of countries, though located on the same continent, added to the growing intrigue and mystery of God's prophetic release.

Soon to follow was a brilliant night-time encounter with a full moon and countless stars in God's miraculous sky. This scene was brought to a marvelous conclusion: Each pinpoint of pulsating light in the sky above was named by its Creator. How could that be? The stars and planets number in hundreds of millions and not all are visible to the human eye!

The question prompted by this prophetic release was, and is perhaps obvious, "How, O Lord, can you keep track of all your creation?"

The answer: As the Maestro's hand lifts His golden baton, so then begins the symphony of creation in all its forms and all of its locations. Sit back and listen. The sounds are celestial! Thank you, Lord.

Biography

Matt is an amazing person with a powerful faith who encourages others. A surgery that went wrong years ago, confined him to a wheel chair. Many days he lives in excruciating pain; yet, he loves the Lord and sketches when he can. He is seventy-seven years old, married forty-eight years to Carol, has three daughters and eight grand-children. He graduated from DePaul University in 1959 and came to Christ in 1982. Thus began his love of drawing, especially of Jesus Christ.

Contact Information

Email: mattclawlor@comcast.net

Jesus forgives our sins and makes us new.

Title: Untitled
Medium: Oil on canvas
Artist: Rosie Martindale

Copyright © 2013 Rosie Martindale. Used with permission.

This painting grew out of my commitment to seek God for personal freedom from the unforgiveness and fears from my past and to engage in life.

I have seen "the light bulb go on" as people get a visual which gives them a reason to never give up, and a hope that they will overcome.

Close up of Rosie Martindale's painting.

Biography

Rosemarie Martindale teaches and creates artwork in between being a wife and mom. Her most current body of work integrates miniature paintings into three-dimensional multimedia constructions which explore and share God's heart. Rosie has been exhibiting publicly for over 18 years, is a member of Christians In the Visual Arts and American Miniature Association. She holds a Master's degree from Governor's State University.

Her work can be seen on her website listed below, and on Fine Arts America.com.

Contact Information

Website: martindaleartventures.weebly.com

Advice

Spend time with the Lord. Enjoy Him. Cultivate the habit of actively listening for Him to speak throughout the day. Journal and refine the ideas He gives until the image can stand alone, needing no verbal explanation. Ask others for input, so you can find out what works and what doesn't.

Rosemarie is writing and illustrating a book called, *Beowulf: Fatherless Prince* It's a story of Beowulf retold in alliterative verse for primary age children. Although Beowulf grows up without his father, other men take a father's interest in him and help the little boy to become an honorable, brave man.

Scripture leads us into wisdom.

Title: Flourishing Palm
Medium: Colored pencils
Artist: Marianne Chen

Copyright 2013 Marianne Chen. Used with permission.

Inspired by Psalm 92, this piece of art illustrates the difference between those who are planted in the House of God (Psalm 92:12a) and those who reject Him (Psalm 92:9b). An individual planted in the house of God is fed and cultivated by God, resulting in his/her full potential — a flourishing palm. Those who choose their own way are like plants in a field that turn into stubble and are burned.

"The righteous will flourish like a palm tree, they will grow like a cedar of Lebanon; planted in the house of the LORD, they will flourish in the courts of our God. They will still bear fruit in old age, they will stay fresh and green, proclaiming, 'The LORD is upright; he is my Rock, and there is no wickedness in him.'" — Psalm 92:12-15

Biography
I was born in 1953, but I've never been older than age 29. I started journaling in 2008 and discovered that the Lord put an artist in me!

Contact Information
Email: prdmm777@gmail.com

Advice
Just go for it!

Yahweh outlines the way.

Title: A Divine Storyboard
Medium: Colored pencils
Artist: Marianne Chen

The Cross, the intersection of history,
Floats on in space and time;
The hinge, between the banishment
    and mystery,
Holds us to God Divine.

A gift to fallen humanity,
Banished from the garden;
Reclaims the soul from calamity;
Covers it with pardon.

So man and woman were banished
    from Eden,
But God did not despair;
Unrolled before the created foundation,
The plans of God — with flair!

A second Adam would suffice,
On Him the burdens fall.
Belief in Him, to be precise,
Will carry the whole ball.

Jesus turns our darkness into light.

Title: Nobody Knows the Trouble I've Seen
Medium: Mixed media
Artist: Tim Botts

This is one of 52 African American spirituals I expressed in calligraphy for the book, *Bound for Glory.* It represents the miracle of these songs — that in spite of the hypocrisy of their "Christian" masters, the slaves came to know and embrace the real Jesus. So that contrast is expressed in descending dark letters against a trembling, but triumphant "Glory Hallelujah."

Tim's book is available on Amazon.com

Biography

Tim Botts studied calligraphy with Arnold Bank at Carnegie-Mellon University as part of his graphic design training. While teaching conversational English in Japan for three years, he was influenced by their rich culture of brush writing.

He designed more than 600 books during his 40 years at Tyndale House Publishers, before retiring in 2012.

He continues to create calligraphic works and to teach calligraphy. He is the artistic director for Masterpiece Ministries, an outreach to high school students in the arts.

He and his wife, Nancy, live in Glen Ellyn, Illinois, and are the parents of three grown children and thirteen grandchildren.

Contact Information

Website: www.timbotts.com

Advice

From the words of Jesus: It is more blessed to give than to receive. Be generous with the gift God has given you.

The Lord makes us strong in our struggles.

Title: Eagle
Medium: Acrylic
Artist: Natalie Totire

It's in the midst of our struggles, that the Lord does amazing things.

Despite trying to forget about art and the need for money, I went to Cosley Zoo to sketch animals. The love of money can thwart even art. And talking about myself, rather than the subject I'm drawing, makes me a boring person.

The focus should be on the subject I'm sketching — the majestic red-tailed hawk with the twinkle in its eyes, and the brightly-colored Baltimore oriole, and the coyote standing peacefully on the log. These things help me forget about what I lack in life.

Each time I observe God's creatures and draw them, I learn something new about the animals and about God. This is a painting of an eagle — one of the many raptures that I draw.

Christ enables us to see beauty.

Title: God's Mighty Raptors
Medium: Acrylic
Artist: Natalie Totire

God's Mighty Raptures is a book idea the Lord put on my heart, as I was sketching birds and animals at Cosley Zoo. I saw such beauty in the red-tailed hawk that I knew I had to write and illustrate a book on raptures.

I plan to market this book to Christian schools and home-schooled children who want to learn about raptures and about God. The book will be published in 2014.

Jesus pulls us out of despair.

Title: Faith
Medium: Colored pencil on cardstock
Artist: Natalie Totire

I created this work of art at the end of 2011. How I came up with this image was a long story. In October, 2011, I was going through a disappointing time as an artist. I was putting in more effort and more money than I was making sales. I was especially excited about a new sequel book I had written, but no one seemed interested in buying it.

I gave into despair, but had to quiet my thoughts and focus on God instead. It was then that God spoke to my heart about having faith. Bible leaders become leaders because of their faith in God, not because of their natural abilities. It is faith that brings maturity in our Christian walk.

God then reminded me that nine years prior, He started to put into my heart a desire to move to Wheaton, Illinois. But for many years it all seemed unlikely to happen.

In 2009, circumstances caused everything to fall in place and it came to pass. I pictured this event as God's helping hand to help me have faith that other unseen promises will take place — including an open door that I would get hired to illustrate children's books, or use my art in some good way to serve God in His time.

I previously drew a pencil sketch of a boy climbing a mountain. That picture grabbed my attention many times while God spoke to my heart. Based on that image, I created this new picture, turning the boy into a girl and adding the hand of Christ reaching down to help with the slippery, steep path.

I posted this picture on Facebook after drawing it, and was surprised by the tremendous response from my friends. One friend, that I had known for a long time, who was not a Christian, said she was so touched by the sketch that she printed it out and hung it on her wall. I had more responses over this picture than any of the illustrations or paintings I previously made to advertise my art.

Biography

I always enjoyed drawing and painting since I was a small child. I optioned an Associate's degree in Early Childhood Education and a Bachelor's Degree in Education Ministries at Moody Bible Institute. Over time, I discovered that my greatest passion was in writing and illustrating children's books.

Contact Information

Website: www.natalietcreations.com   Email: NTcreations@live.com

Advice

Remember that being an artist is not an easy road. We will all face failure and we all need God's help. At times, art may be used to make money. Other times it is used plainly to serve and to minister. If God speaks to your heart, and the best way to describe what He shows you is through images, do not hesitate to get out your paper and start drawing. What God leads you to create will always, in the long run, minister to someone.

God places good ideas on our heart.

Title: Scarubery Woods
Medium: Watercolor
Artist: Natalie Totire

The Lord gave Natalie an idea for writing and illustrating a fantasy story for children ages eight to twelve, about an imaginary world with imaginary creatures that represent the human race. Because it's a make-believe world, the story transcends cultures and presents the gospel message in an interesting manner.

Natalie's book, "Scarubery Woods is available on www.lulu.com as a paperback, and on Amazon Kindle as an e-book. It contains delightful black and while illustrations.

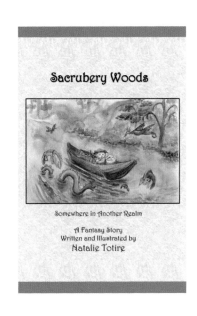

Sacrubery Woods

Somewhere in Another Realm

A Fantasy Story
Written and Illustrated by
Natalie Totire

Yahweh releases the prophetic.

Title: Frames
Medium: Mixed media
Artist: Lyn Rowley

The frames I created for my grandchildren grew out of prophetic words that were received before they were born.

When my daughter was pregnant with her first child, my granddaughter Aurelia, both of us received words and dreams regarding the plan and purpose for this child. I am prophetic, my daughter is very prophetic, and we both heard clearly that Aurelia would be even more prophetic.

Shortly after her birth she was having some health issues. I asked a powerful man of God to pray for her. He prophesied that Aurelia was a "little bird with a big voice." And furthermore, she would be able to reach her generation for Christ. She is a prophet of the Lord. Her frame is done in blues — the color of the living water of the Holy Spirit.

(More frames on next page)

Yahweh releases the prophetic. (continued)

Title: Frames
Medium: Mixed media
Artist: Lyn Rowley

When Elliana was born, both her mother and I had been hearing that she would be an intercessor. But I felt that there was much more than we were seeing. As I was driving to the hospital to witness her birth, I passed the town's high school. Their mascot is "Warriors." Jesus spoke at that moment and said that Ellie would be a warrior for the Lord. She would not only pray and intercede, but that she would stand on the mountains and take back the land for Lord. She would declare and do the Lord's work in love.

When I made the frame, the mountain at the bottom was in place. However, by the time the present was open, the mountain had shifted. I have not fixed this! I believe that Jesus is saying that even when the mountains shake and fall, Ellie will stand in the high places and take back the land. Her frame is done in pinks — the color of Love.

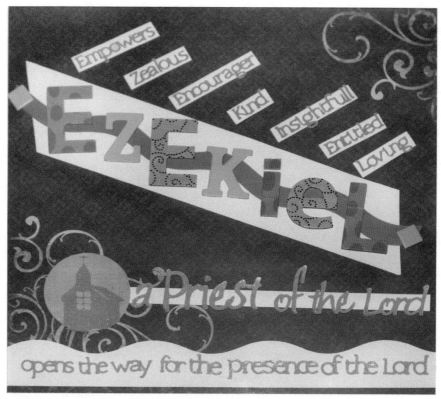

Ezekiel's birth was foretold more than a year before he was born. Gwen, his mother, was told that she would conceive on Rosh Hashanah and confirm the pregnancy on Yom Kippur. The baby would be a boy and his name would be Ezekiel. He would be a priest of the Lord.

I heard that he would be able to create "open heavens" that would usher people into the presence of God. Before he was born, I received the descriptive words from the letters of his name. Each of these words describe character qualities that Zeke has been given to fulfill his destiny. His frame is primarily green — the color of eternal life and growth.

Biography

I am a wife, mother and grandmother, and most importantly, a Christ follower. I love photos. In the last 15 years I've been an avid scrapbooker, cherishing the idea of preserving memories and traditions through pictures and journaling. I've kept a private journal since 1988 and love to see how Jesus speaks through this. These frames are a combination of prophetic words I've received with my scrapbooking for my grandchildren.

I worked with children for most of my life and enjoy seeing the freedom and joy that is expressed through paper, glue and inspiration. These pictures have brought me that same freedom and joy.

Contact Information

Email: lynrowley@hotmail.com
Blog: lynrowley.blogspot.com

Advice

Think outside of the box when it comes to creating. There is no right or wrong way to create — so just do it!

The Lord turns our sorrow into joy!

Title: Julia
Medium: Acrylic on cold press paper
Artist: Mary Sheesley-Warburton

"Julia" is a painting of a street child — representative of the many street children my husband and I saw on our mission trips to China. While Bob and I were teaching language and literature classes at Shandong University, the real "Julia" came into our lives. One of Bob's married students invited us to a special dinner at a restaurant in downtown Jinan. At the dinner was another young couple — the parents of a little girl we had heard about.

As I watched the little girl dressed in her very best, I thought about the promises of God — that He would continue to make His Name known among the many people in China. Then the little girl's mother turned to me and said, "Mary, I would like to request a favor from you. Our daughter has a traditional Chinese name. But we would like her to have a special Christian name — one she can use in her school and community, and one she can pronounce."

Immediately, the name "Julia" came to my mind. This was my mother's name. She was a precious woman who loved Jesus, and I wanted the little girl to have the name of someone who lived to please the Lord.

Bob wrote a poem to commemorate this happy occasion, amidst a background of stress and sorrow in a land of struggle experienced by many street children. To better understand the poem you need to know that Shandong University is affectionately called "Shanda." The common trees on the campus are called "The Weeping Scholar Trees." Their bark is black, gnarled and jagged with crooked limbs that give them a ragged look. They remind the students that their scholarly life is often full of woe, subject to the winds of pressure, testing, competition and the fragile task of survival. Students shed tears under the great pressure to succeed in their studies.

"Julia" by Bob Warburton

They came in Advent's hope – father, mother, child, on Shanda's campus of snow-cover greens, under winter's Weeping Scholar Trees yet dressed in frail vines of tear-shaped leaves; for their only daughter-child — ever they came to endow her with a sacred newborn name.

So Mary named her "Julia," Godchild, dearest Advent child come, China's child of promise. And Mary painted her so, as drawn by grace, as etched on the Savior's heart by love, for thus to come in peace and joy to Him, precious Advent Savior come, come also now for us.

Biography

Visual art has been a life-long pursuit for Mary, and at the age of 87, she still paints and prepares for shows. She has painted in ten different countries, and works in pen, pencil, watercolors, acrylics, charcoal, pastels, linoleum block prints, Chinese brush painting on rice paper and encaustics (an ancient medium of pigmented bees wax). She has exhibited her work in the USA and overseas and is a member of numerous art associations. Her subject material includes portraits, still life, landscapes, flowers, various thematic motifs — both traditional and abstract, and personal memoirs. Mary graduated from Houghton College.

Contact Information

Email: maryshewarburton@aol.com

Advice

Never give up. God is our everlasting strength and hope. He will help you create. We are made in His image and when we make things, we are following the Master Painter's design.

In HIS Light we see light.

Title: Untitled
Medium: Digital photography
Artist: Ruth LaSure

"For with You is the fountain of life; in Your light we see light." — Psalm 36: 9 (NKJV)

Three consecutive mornings I received Scriptures concerning trusting God and dwelling in the shelter or shadow of His wings. Dwelling means to live there. Under His wings you shall take refuge, Psalm 91:1-4; I will trust in the shelter of your wings, Psalm 61:1-4; hide me under the shadow of your wings, Psalm 17:8-9.

I think this relates to this piece of prophetic art, as does Psalm 55, which is a prayer of trust, knowing the streets are filled with horrors; knowing that there are dangers everywhere, from within as well as without, things that can break trust.

David begins by saying, "Give ear to my prayer, O God. And do not hide from my supplication." In verse 22 he says, "Cast your burden on the Lord, and he shall sustain you. He shall never permit the righteous to be moved."

And finally I feel the art imaging this wonderful Scripture passage in Psalm 36: 7-9, "How precious is Your lovingkindness, O God! Therefore the children of men put their trust under the shadow of Your wings. They are abundantly satisfied with the fullness of Your house. And You give them drink from the river of Your pleasures. For with You is the fountain of life; in Your light we see light."

Scriptures quotes are from the New King James Version.

Biography

Ruth LaSure studied drawing and painting for three years at the American Academy of Art in Chicago, Illinois. She took classes in sculpture and various areas of intaglio printmaking at College of Du Page in Glen Ellyn, and Elgin Community College in Elgin, Illinois. She has also taken various classes at the Du Page Art League, the Palette and Chisel in Chicago, and other private studies and workshops.

Contact Information

Email: cooks.gallery@yahoo.com

Advice

Plan to be a life-long learner. If you desire to make a career of visual art then get all the training that you can, especially in drawing — using many different tools, such as charcoal, graphite, pen and ink, silverpoint, and etching needle. And yet the skill is only built by diligent practice. Think of a concert musician who spends many hours honing his skills.

The second area of utmost importance is good design. Even color choices have a design element to them. Look, look, look, at nature, at man-made structures, at books of art, and in museums — there is an art to seeing.

This is the most important advice. With age come some wisdom, and although all that I wrote above is true, it is not what I have done, or not entirely, I confess. Early, as a little girl, I showed an aptitude for drawing, and later for color harmony, and design. I did many things connected to the arts, but did not go to art classes, or attempt any visual art until mid-life. Then, after wonderful training and strong encouragement I allowed disruptions to become a deterrent to the dream I felt God had placed in my spirit. I allowed my feelings to droop, not trusting completely that God still has a plan for me that could include the dream placed into my care so long ago.

There is nothing that surpasses the love of God for us. The possibilities are limitless when we truly place our hand in His each day — one day at a time.

Jesus adds color and completeness to our lives.

Title: Untitled
Medium: Mixed media
Artist: Ruth LaSure

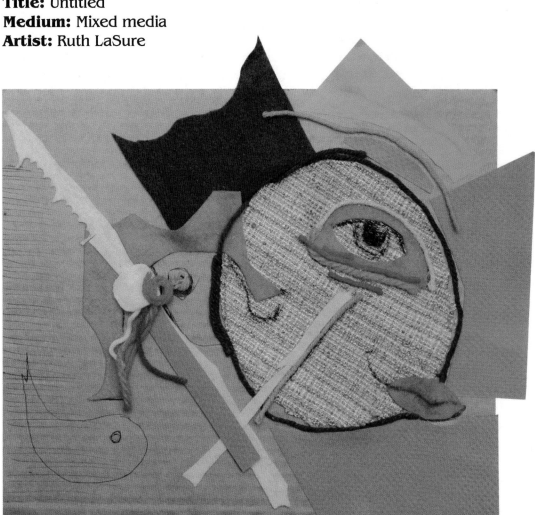

Copyright 2009 Ruth LaSure. Used with permission.

I believe this spontaneous piece of prophetic collage art shows where I am, at the moment. It is unfinished, but the fragments of color on the right half of the piece show a future full of development and full of blooming color as I allow God to direct me. The left corner shows a faintly drawn fish midst emptiness. The image next to the fish is chaotic, but pulling up from the chaos is a golden Sword of the Spirit.

The right two thirds of the piece have a reference to the "Eye of God," with a golden crown. There are splashes of bright and subdued colors and textures with ink drawn parts.

The Lord holds us firmly in place.

Title: Holding Steady
Medium: Pencil
Artist: Rosalinda V. Lopez

In spite of feeling lost, shunned and rejected at times, I'm actually a beautiful creature like this bird, firmly gripping hold of the branch. Other branches that crisscross in my life, try to entrap me. But I can sit steadily on the right branch.

Biography
I was born in the USA. After living in Mexico for 20 years and giving birth to six sons, my husband and I returned the United States to finish raising our boys. While in Mexico, I served as a worship leader. Today, I'm stepping forth in my calling as an artist, poet and songwriter.

Advice
Go with your heart and ask God for His guidance so you know how to convey His message in your art.

Contact Information
Email: rosalin53@hotmail.com

The Lord rescues us.

Title: Storm at Sea
Medium: Pastel
Artist: Rosalinda V. Lopez

This piece of art was an image the Lord gave Rosalinda. Little did Rosalinda know, that as she sketched the picture, an Arizona family was lost at sea.

When Rosalinda read their story in the newspaper she was stunned. She learned that weeks after the family left the United States, storms damaged their small boat and left them adrift. They were rescued when a fishing vessel picked them up and took them to Chile.

She turned her pencil sketch into a pastel drawing, and shares her poem, "YOU are a Star."

YOU are a Star
Like a Diamond in the Sky.
Like a Lantern in the dark,
YOU will always be my Guide at night.

I stumble, I fall,
My path has been broken.
My hopes and illusions,
Have from me been taken.

I sit on the shore,
Looking out at the horizon.
The sun is changing colors,
As it slips in the ocean.

I row out to Sea,
The waves crashing around me.
The thunder and lightning,
And darkness is engulfing.

The ocean is vast,
My small boat is sinking.
Not far in the distance,
A lighthouse is blinking.

I row frantically,
High waves are all around me.
Suddenly appearing,
A fisherman saves me.

HIS lantern I see,
I steer in his direction.
Taking his hand in mine,
I am in his protection.

YOU are a Star.

Copyright © April 2013 Rosalinda V. Lopez

Jesus identifies with our pain.

Title: Untitled
Medium: Pen and Ink
Artist: Rosalinda V. Lopez

I sketched this image of Jesus during a difficult time in my life. Christ identifies with our pain, and I wanted to portray His human side. He knows what it feels like to be betrayed. He knows what if feels like to be sad.

Always know that when you are sad or facing troubles you are not facing them alone. Jesus is with you. And He feels what you feel.

Copyright © 2013 Rosalinda V. Lopez Used with permission.

Christ gives us a new perspective.

Title: Tetons in Perspective
Medium: Digital Photography
Artist: Becky Jane Davis

As I visited the national parks, the Lord gave me a word or phrase for each park. My job was to find a picture and Bible passage to go with the words. For Grand Teton National Park, the word was, "Perspective." It's all about perspective. Up high there is a different beauty. At our level, there is beauty as well, but the perspective is different.

Do we look at the flowers, or the mountains? Do our eyes focus on the trees or the grassy plain? Do we look for elk in the trees or goats on the mountain ridges?

The question we should ask is, where is God looking? What is His perspective? What does He see? The whole or the parts? Often, we get our eyes fixed on one thing, when God would have us look at something else entirely.

Ask God now, what do you want me to see in this image? What is your perspective on the mountains and flowers? What are you telling me today about what you see and how you want me to see things?

"For my thoughts are not your thoughts, neither are your ways my ways," declares the LORD. "As the heavens are higher than the earth, so are my ways higher than your ways and my thoughts than your thoughts." Isaiah 55:8-9

"I lift up my eyes to the mountains — where does my help come from? My help comes from the LORD, the Maker of heaven and earth." — Psalm 121:1-2

Biography

I can't remember when I didn't have a camera in my hand. My first camera was around the age of seven. In high school, I got my first SLR camera. Later, after college, I upgraded to a new Minolta. Today, I use a Nikon DSLR.

I've taken classes at the local community college and I've almost completed my certificate in photography technology.

Over the years, I've tried my hand at portraiture, event photography and photo restoration. My current focus is travel photo-graphy and fine arts photography. Occasionally, I still do photo restoration or an event. But what I'd really like is for someone to pay for me to travel and take pictures of the Lord's creation.

Becky is planning a book that focuses on images from National Parks and the words that The Lord has spoken to her about each of the parks. When the book is ready, she will announce it on her website and blog.

Contact Information
Website: beckyjanedavis.com   Blog: beckyjanedavis.com/blog

Advice
It's not about the camera, it's about your eye and how you frame what you see. It's not about how many megapixels you have. It's about how you see light and how you see people. The best advice I ever had was to take an empty, 4" x 6," matt board frame, hold it up and look at the world through this frame, turning it vertical, horizontal and angled to see what things look like when framed. Composition is so important in an image — what you see and where the elements are placed. Also, remember that often the best time to take pictures is right after the sun rises and right before it sets.

God is a mighty fortress.

Title: Fortress Walk
Medium: Digital Photography
Artist: Becky Jane Davis

All along the Danube River you can see old fortresses built high on rock promontories where land could be defended from the enemy. In Passau, Germany, the Veste Oberhaus, built in 1219, rises over 300 feet above the Danube. It has been partially restored and you can walk through the fortress to see what it must have been like in the middle ages to depend on a fortress for protection.

The fortress could house, feed and protect the entire population at a time of war. A wall surrounds the complex, with defensive and offensive battlements strategically placed around the perimeter. There are towers, and as Christians, we like to think of God as a strong tower (the righteous run into Him and are saved). But there is so much more to a fortress, than a tower.

Connecting all the battlements, housing, settlements and regal courts were walkways like this one. This path is narrow with a stone wall on the left to provide protection so no enemy can disturb the walk. On the right, soft grasses make you feel that you could lie down and rest or relax in safety, if you wanted. Following the path beyond the grasses, were the merchants, homes, servants and courts. Because you were never alone in the fortress, there was always help, if you needed it, and always someone to talk to.

Up ahead is a small, narrow gate — because the fortress needs to be defensible, in case of attack. In times of peace, people need to be able to come to court or go into the market below, but it is narrow, so only one or two can pass at a time. Beyond the world outside the fortress, is the city below and the mountains in the distance.

The fortress and the narrow path remind us of God and what He says of His protection and plans for us. His plan is for us to seek shelter in Him and to stand on the Rock so we are stable in our walk with Him.

Instead of looking at narrow gates as restrictive, we should see that they are for our protection from the enemy — to keep us safe, and on the right path. We are never alone, because He is always with us. He will provide everything we need, both in times of war and in times of peace. We can rest safely, knowing He will protect us.

"The LORD is my rock, my fortress, and my deliverer; my God is my rock, in whom I take refuge, my shield, and the horn of my salvation, my stronghold."
— Psalm 18:2

"Enter through the narrow gate. For wide is the gate and broad is the road that leads to destruction, and many enter through it." — Matthew 7:13

The Lord helps us to forgive.

Title: Hope and Forgiveness
Medium: Mixed media
Artist: Donna Lehrer

This piece of art was created in 2013, in memory of the Ukrainian Farmers and their families who lost their lives during the terrible Holodomor-Famine-Genocide that took place from 1932 to 1933.

Each element of this art has a special meaning. The shock of wheat was harvested from a wheat field in Big Rock, Illinois, where Donna raises sheep and produce with her husband Scott, and their two children. The shock is lovingly wrapped in a piece of embroidery created by Anna, a Ukrainian relative.

There are three pieces of silk paintings. The first one is Ukrainian for "Death by Starvation." This banner is placed on top of a piece of linen similar to that produced by the Ukrainian farmers. The two others silk pieces are Hope and Forgiveness. The silk painting technique was chosen since it dates back to the Czar's family. The words are placed on pieces of felted wool from the artist's flock of sheep. Donna's grandmother also raised sheep in the Ukraine.

The gold cross that surrounds the word Hope is from Donna's mother, Nadja. Nadja means "faith." It has a special significance, since it was blessed by the Bishop of their church.

Faith is what gets you though life's tragedies. Donna realized this early in life. She was born after her brother, Michael, died at the young age of 6. Losing a child at any age is devastating to a mother.

The two photos of the starving children were added to remind us of how precious life is. They were placed on top of an antique handkerchief which would have dried many a tears from their mother's eyes.

The entire piece is framed in old weathered barn wood from a 100 year old barn on the artist's farm property. The weathered wood symbolizes how we can weather life's storms if we have a sense of faith.

The backdrop for the piece is brown burlap material. This would have been similar to the material used to store the grains and potato crops the Ukrainian farmers so lovingly produced that were so violently destroyed by the evils of the Stalin government. A white felted dove flies above the sad memories to provide hope for future generations of Ukrainian farmers.

As hard as it is to forgive, hope and forgiveness are the only ways we can be set free from the horrors of genocide in this world. Jesus forgave us, and He calls us to forgive others.

Biography

Donna Lehrer was born in a town outside Philadelphia. Her grandparents were Ukrainian immigrants who settled in upstate Pennsylvania in the early 1900's. She is now living in farm country outside of Chicago, raising sheep and working with her daughter, Natasha, on their small farm and in their fiber studio. She is passionate about being the voice for the small farmer.

Contact Information

Email: info@esthersplacefibers.com

Her goal is to raise awareness of the past and current plight of the small farmer in America and around the world. She hopes her new developments in the art world will help make a difference for the future of all farmers in the world — to not forget the tragedies of the past, but learn from them.

Advice

Keep on creating from inspiration from our Creator and don't let the world's negative judgment discourage your creativity!

Jesus calls us to be fishers of men.

Title: Fisher of Men
Medium: Pencil
Artist: "Grace"

God calls HIS artists to be fishers of men through art. And that's exactly what happened to Jacqueline Martorano.

A few weeks before the 2013 Karitos Christian Arts Conference, she began a portrait of her daughter. It wasn't coming out the way she wanted it to look, so she asked the Holy Spirit to help her. He did. Note the light found in the eyes, as the eyes are the windows to a person's soul. (Matthew 6:22)

After Karitos, Jacki was released into prophetic art — totally yielding herself and her pencil sketching to the guidance and direction of the Holy Spirit. She created art with God as a form of worship.

Notice the fish in the net. The more you look, the more fish you see.

Five months later, after praying with her son when he asked for prayer to receive the baptism of the Holy Spirit, he was also released into prophetic art.

"Come, follow me" Jesus said, "and I will send you out to fish for people."
— Matthew 4:19

"The eye is the lamp of the body. If your eyes are healthy, your whole body will be full of light." — Matthew 6:22

The Lord is our refuge.

Title: Psalm 36:7-9
Medium: Colored paper
Artist: "Grace"

Many images can be seen in this paper collage: a river, a tree with abundant, green foliage, a crown, sunshine and rocks. But what cannot be seen, until you lift up the hand-shaped wing, is a baby bird sheltered under the safety of God's protection.

When Jacki was creating this piece of art, the Lord kept telling her again and again, "I want My Hand over you."

"He made my mouth like a sharpened sword, in the shadow of his hand he hid me; he made me into a polished arrow and concealed me in his quiver."
— Isaiah 49:2

"But the pot he was shaping from the clay was marred in his hands; so the potter formed it into another pot, shaping it as seemed best to him.

"Then the word of the Lord came to me. He said, 'Can I not do with you, house of Israel, as this potter does?' declares the Lord. 'Like clay in the hand of the potter, so are you in my hand, house of Israel.'"
— Jeremiah 18:4-6

"How priceless is your unfailing love, O God! People take refuge in the shadow of your wings. They feast on the abundance of your house; you give them drink from your river of delights. For with you is the fountain of life; in your light we see light." — Psalm 36:7-9

"I have put my words in your mouth and covered you with the shadow of my hand— I who set the heavens in place, who laid the foundations of the earth, and who say to Zion, 'You are my people.'"
—Isaiah 51:16

Biography
"Grace" currently resides in northern Illinois. GOD has blessed her with two children. Although she dabbled in art in her early years, she was not blessed with prophetic artistry until she attended the 2013 Karitos Christian Art Conference. GOD now works through her in amazing ways. When Jacki asked the Lord how she should sign her art, the word, "Grace" came to mind — her work is created by God's grace.

Advice
The advice I would give is to stay in the Lord, for through HIM all things are possible!

Jesus wraps us in the softness of His love.

Title: Untitled
Medium: Fabric and trim
Artist: Rachael Weidman

The sun, in this piece of fabric art, represents Christianity and the Light of God reaching and spreading out into others, lighting up the world with His warmth. The heart represents our heart with the Holy Spirit in us and God's Hands (the yellow yarn) holding us. The green cloth shows His gentleness and His softness wrapping around us, protecting us. The dark flower in the lower right corner is us. Even though we have sin and darkness, God's Light still shines through us so we can follow in His footsteps.

Biography
I'm Rachael Weidman and I'm thirteen years old. I love to do art! It's amazing to see what God can do through anyone, no matter how old you are.

Advice
Just let God take the reins and work through you.

Jesus guides our every footstep.

Title: God's Family Path
Medium: Mixed media
Artist: Cathie Zurek-Geske

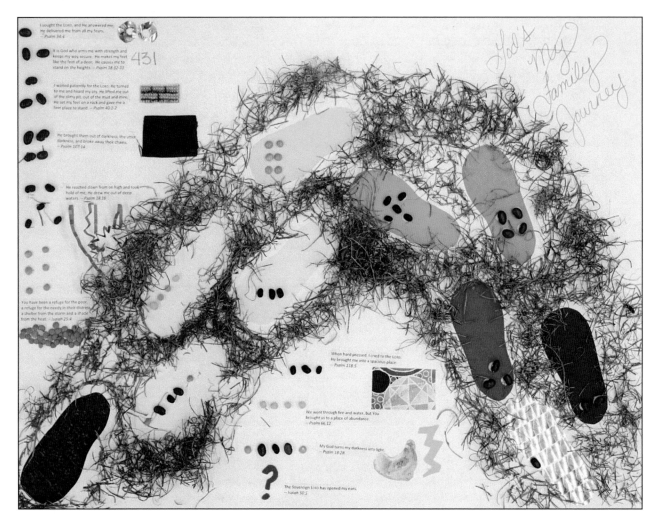

Scripture Cathie used for her art map:

I sought the LORD, and he answered me; he delivered me from all my fears. — Psalm 34:4

It is God who arms me with strength and keeps my way secure. He makes my feet like the feet of a deer; he causes me to stand on the heights. — Psalm 18:32-33

I waited patiently for the LORD; he turned to me and heard my cry. He lifted me out of the slimy pit, out of the mud and mire; he set my feet on a rock and gave me a firm place to stand. — Psalm 40:1-2

He brought them out of darkness, the utter darkness, and broke away their chains. — Psalm 107:14

He reached down from on high and took hold of me; he drew me out of deep waters. — Psalm 18:16

You have been a refuge for the poor, a refuge for the needy in their distress, a shelter from the storm and a shade from the heat. — Isaiah 25:4

When hard pressed, I cried to the LORD; he brought me into a spacious place. — Psalm 118:5

You let people ride over our heads; we went through fire and water, but you brought us to a place of abundance. — Psalm 66:12

You, LORD, keep my lamp burning; my God turns my darkness into light. — Psalm 18:28

The Sovereign LORD has opened my ears. — Isaiah 50:5

This art map records my journey for the past seven years, since I got married. It starts out with a footprint that is representative of the first home my husband and I lived in, and chronicles both my station in life and my faith walk.

At that time, while I was what I considered a devout Christian, looking back, it was more about me than God. As I journeyed through various other homes and life situations, it became less about me and more about God and His plan for me.

Each footprint is something that reminds me of the particular station I was at. For example, the interlocking rings is when we got married. The crinkly paper tendrils represent the mold growing out in fingers from the walls in the house in Racine, Wisconsin, after the basement flooded.

The open (void) footprint is where I hope to be at some point in my faith journey — where my will and what I want is void, and it is all about what God would have for my life and that it's all about HIM!!!

To date, we have lived in thirteen different homes in eight years. God has become more and more important, and His will is so much better than my own for my life and for the life of my family.

Hindsight is always 20/20 and it's important — of the utmost of importance — to look around you at all times. While it's hard to see the Benevolent Master's Plan in the moment, reflection shows clearly His plan in everything, even the perceived difficulty. And while looking back shows growth and His plan unfolding in our past, it's very important to pray in the moment, discern each step, and proceed forward with reckless abandon when we receive marching orders from Jesus!

Through all of this, I have learned to just trust the leading of the Holy Spirit and move as He tells me to. And even when I do not understand in the moment, He is gracious enough to let me take a glimpse into my past to see how He carried me and directed me. And this always gives me a boost into my future with Him.

Biography
My name is Catherine Michelle Geske (nee Zurek). I am 36 years old and relatively new to the prophetic arts. I was born and raised in the Northwest suburbs of Chicago and currently live in the Rockford, Illinois area with my husband Steve and four teenagers.

Contact Information
Email: email: mrspastor1977@yahoo.com
Facebook: Cathie Zurek-Geske

Advice
Don't ever be afraid to express yourself as Holy Spirit leads you.

Christ calls us to love one another.

Title: Blue Morning Glories and Magnolia
Medium: Pencils and colored pencils
Artist: Rose Calkins

Rose uses whatever tool she has on hand, when the Holy Spirit prompts her to show love to a member of her family.

The blue flowers were sketched at a restaurant with my son Tony, when he was 12, after he had assisted me with a Saturday art class I taught to toddlers and their parents. As we waited for our meal, I was enjoying this beautiful time with my son that blossomed into this piece of art for him. It was a cluster of Blue Morning Glories with a special message, "I love you Tony! Love forever — Mom xxx...ooo... Live a joyful life!"

He smiled and took the artwork. I felt very blessed. Even though I probably used my entire earnings on this shared meal. This simple picture — a gift from mother to son — was to be multiplied on many levels later on. It was a loaves and fishes type of multiplication.

After a visit to my son at the Masterpiece Summer Arts Camp in Kentucky, I headed back to the hotel just outside of Nashville. As I was getting out of our car, I walked passed a grouping of four trees that lined the parkway, and noticed a single white blossom on one of the trees. I reached up and drew in the heady, aromatic scent of the magnolia. I stood there for a good minute or two with my nose buried into the blossom, inhaling its fragrance. Then I looked up into the clear blue sky and asked my mom if this is what heaven's scent was like. (My mom recently arrived there three months earlier, on her 91st birthday.)

For the next two days, I took every opportunity to deeply inhale the beautiful scent of the magnolia blossom. Early on the last day, as we were packing the car to leave, another magnolia flower blossomed in the glory of God's morning.

When I arrived home, I felt compelled to create a magnolia blossom in the same simple manner in which I had created the blue morning glories. I dug out my art pencils, but did not need many colors to draw it, since the pure, white blossom was the color of the paper.

The years between the creation of the morning glories drawing and the creation of the magnolia art, was a very challenging time for our family. But God is always faithful and present as He opens our eyes and hearts to see His lavish beauty — in us, in His world, and especially in the loving life restoring creation of His Son.

Biography
I am a writer, publisher, singer, and a dabbler in drawing, theater arts, and photography. I'm a mother of four, which gives me the most perspiration and inspiration. I'm also a teacher, and thus a learner. I taught high school English, writing workshops, art classes, theater workshops, religious education, and at one time, aerobics. I'm a founder of "The DuPage Writers Group" that meets monthly — to critique our work and publish an annual literary journal.

Contact Information
Email: rosecalkins@comcast.net
www.facebook.com/rosemarycalkinsauthor

Advice
Take the time to make your art. Enjoy creating it. It's a thank you to God when you open and use His kind and generous gift, which He specifically gave to you.

Rose shows us the importance of taking time to love our children (and grandchildren) by spending one-on-one time with them, doing things together, involving them in the workshops or art that we do, and using the talents God gave us to bless them and show them that we care — even if the only thing we have available to draw on is a napkin at a restaurant.

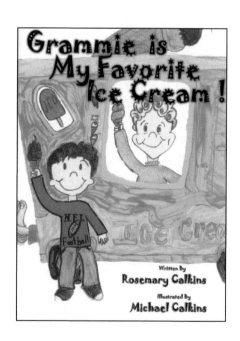

Grammie is My Favorite Ice Cream! is a tender, touching story about the deep love a grandson has for his grandmother. This 34 page book was written by Rose Calkins and illustrated by her younger son, Michael. Together, they colored the pictures and had fun bringing Michael's idea and sketches to reality. For information on how to order this book, send an email to Rose.

The Lord brings us into His Light

Title: Angel Light
Medium: Digital art
Artist: Lynn Zuk-Lloyd

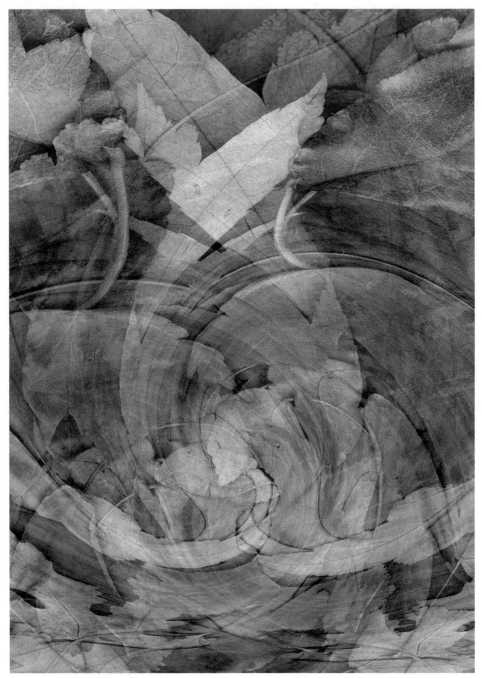

When praying about what image to use for the cover of this book, the Lord brought this piece of art to mind. Christ is bringing light into our understanding. HE is blessing HIS artists with new insights and calling prophetic imagery to come forth. HE is pouring out blessings from Heaven and enabling us to receive them. How awesome! How powerful! How wonderful! For these are the days when art is a tool the Lord uses to comfort, heal, strengthen and restore.

I created this piece of art in one of those "learning by playing" times where I was experimenting with filters and effects on the computer. I worked for a long time blending layers and digitally manipulating the art to create something pleasing to the eye. When I printed it out, my husband looked at it upside down and discovered Heavenly lights and an angel. Wow! God was creating art with me and I didn't even know it!

What makes this piece of art so powerful, is that it visually represents what the Lord is not only doing in my life, but also in the lives of His people — turning us 180 degrees. What I thought were right-side-up thoughts and correct actions, were actually upside down reasoning and self-centered thinking. Jesus is shifting everything to line up with HIS Kingdom and HIS ways! And HE is using prophetic art as a means to do this!

Blessing

May the exuberant love of the Father wash away every hesitancy, doubt and fear.

May a new boldness in faith spring forth in you with a powerful determination to fulfill the longings the Lord placed in your heart.

May the authority Jesus Christ gave you, to trample on snakes and scorpions and to overcome all the power of the enemy (Luke 10:19), become evident in everything you do this year.

About the author.

Lynn Zuk-Lloyd is an artist, author and motivational speaker who lives in the Midwest with her novelist husband, Paul R. Lloyd. She understands the power of pictures, and uses her art, as directed by the Lord, in delightful, interactive ways.

Her presentations, workshops, and newsletters combine words with art to encourage, uplift and strengthen the body of Christ. She welcomes opportunities to speak, teach and also lead prophetic art workshops. Her biography is on page 59.

This painting is just one of the many pieces of art the Lord prompts Lynn to use when speaking. It has been shown at luncheons, ministries, Christian business groups, job clubs, and on-stage at the Karitos Christian Arts Conference.

You can sign up for Lynn's free encouragement email newsletter on www.promisegarden.com and received "*12 Secrets to Thriving in the Desert Moments of our Lives*" as a free gift.

Lynn's contact information:
Website: www.promisegarden.com
Email: lynn@promisegarden.com
Blog: http://encouragementlady.blogspot.com

More books by Lynn Zuk-Lloyd

Books with Prophetic Art, Writing, Scripture and Encouragement

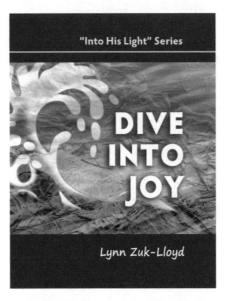

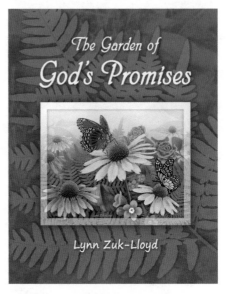

Dive into Joy!

Lynn compiled a collection of uplifting art, stories, reflections and inspiration that she wrote and illustrated. She shares her discovery of stepping into the joy of Jesus in delightful and exciting ways after learning that joy, like happiness, is a choice. This book can be used as a devotional, and has space to enter your own thoughts. Available on Amazon.com

The Garden of God's Promises

Using exquisitely drawn, full-color art and tender, God inspired stories, Lynn offers stepping stones of encouragement for Christians facing worry, fear and stress, or who simply need a place to rest. Her book contains 40 illustrations, 40 stories and over 100 Scripture promises to bless, strengthen and uplift. Available on Amazon.com.

Children's Book

Christmas in North Woods:
12 Stories of Joy and Celebration

Olive Ostrich visits her friends in North Woods. She wants to help them get ready for Christmas. But why does she hide her head in a hole? Will she be brave enough to sled down Scary Hill? And what surprise is hidden in the manger on Christmas Day?

These fun, entertaining stories are written for children ages 5 to 8, but the art and merriment of the adventures can be enjoyed by people of all age.

Available on Amazon.com

Inspirational Non-fiction

Surviving Tough Times: Receiving God's Promises by Letting Go of What We Cling To

Using light-hearted illustrations, thought-provoking ideas and quotes from multiple sources, Lynn reminds us that no problem is too big, too deep, too wide or too far removed to separate us from the love of God and His ability to help us overcome. Available on www.promisegarden.com

Awaken Me! Crying Out for More of the Lord

Are you ready for a spiritual journey that awakens you to the splendor and majesty of the Lord? Experience the joy, freedom and glory that comes from praising and calling out to the Lord from the depths of your heart. This unique type of devotional offers opportunities for imaginative journaling. Available on Amazon.com

Awaken Me! 40 Day Challenge

Are you ready for an exciting, vibrant relationship with Jesus Christ? Do you want to learn how to delight yourself in the Lord more often? Take the Awaken Me! 40 Day Challenge and experience how amazing, how all-encompassing, and complete God's love is for you. Available on www.promisegarden.com and soon on Amazon.com

Fiction

Short Fiction E-Stories

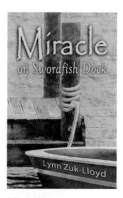

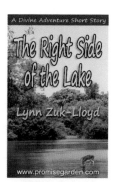

Miracle on Swordfish Dock

A novel about a divine encounter, where the most unlikely person finds herself in the most unusual place, with the most mystifying stranger. Available on Amazon.

Underwater Parallax

The Right Side of the Lake

Would you like to go on an adventure with Jesus? Let Lynn take your imagination on a delightful journey that portrays Christ's amazing love in unique ways. Her e-stories are available on Amazon.com

More great books from Promisegarden.com

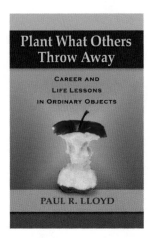

**Plant What Others Throw Away
by Paul R. Lloyd**

Using ordinary, everyday objects, Paul shows how a proper view of success allows you to live in balance with God's call on your life as well as your need to earn an income. This book contains insightful tips and Scriptural quotes on keeping focused and pushing forward. Available on promisegarden.com and soon on Amazon.com

**Fulfillment
by Paul R. Lloyd**

Do you like being scared? This novel about the Christmas story is like nothing you've ever read. Mary's engagement to Joseph should have been joyful, but the secret concerning the baby in her womb catches the attention of evil bent on destroying her. It's fast and intense — spiritual warfare at its best! Available on Amazon.com

Promisegarden.com

DISCOVERING GOD'S PROMISES THROUGH THE ARTS

www.promisegarden.com